FILING BUSINESS NAMES

SECOND EDITION

Simon A. Duchan

Assistant to the Superintendent
Bronx High Schools
Bronx, New York

Robert A. Schultheis

Professor of Business Education and
Administrative Services
Southern Illinois University
Edwardsville, Illinois

Published by

Y14   **SOUTH-WESTERN PUBLISHING CO.**

CINCINNATI   WEST CHICAGO, ILL.   DALLAS   PELHAM MANOR, N.Y.   PALO ALTO, CALIF.

PREFACE

Book 2, *FILING BUSINESS NAMES*, teaches students how to index, code, and alphabetize business names. To help students move smoothly from indexing the names of people to indexing and coding business names, students begin with business names that use the full name of a person. Students then learn to index, code, and alphabetize many other types of business names. *FILING BUSINESS NAMES* is designed to provide mastery of indexing and coding while students work on their own, with a minimum of teacher direction and instruction. The vocabulary level is controlled, which eliminates obstacles to the learning of filing skills.

Part 1: *Filing Business Names Containing Full Personal Names* teaches how to file business names that include the name of a person. Prefixed names, compound last names, and names that include the kind of business are covered.

Part 2: *Filing Business Names with Descriptive Words or Personal Names* covers names with only one part of a person's name, compound business names, and names that do not include a person's name.

Part 3: *Filing Business Names with Connectors or Possessives* provides explanation and practice in the indexing, coding, and alphabetizing of names with connective words commonly used in business names, as well as business names with possessives.

Part 4: *Filing Other Business Names* presents the indexing, coding, and alphabetizing of special types of business names, such as those with abbreviations, numbers, names written as one or two words, and compound geographic names.

Part 5: *Filing Government, Bank, and Chain Store Business Names* covers types of business names that require special indexing and coding rules.

The method of presentation which was developed in Book 1 is continued in Book 2:

(a) A simple, easy-to-understand explanation of indexing rule.
(b) An illustrative problem, with the answer provided, which demonstrates the rule.
(c) A ''practice'' problem, without the answer, is presented for solution by the students. The problem is of the same type and difficulty as the illustrative problem.
(d) A series of different types of problems, covering the same indexing rule is then presented. These illustrative problems permit students to transfer the indexing rule to a different filing situation and to increase their understanding of the rule. Practice in coding business names is also provided.

Each section concludes with an Integrated Practice problem and a summary of what has been learned. The Integrated Practice problem includes the types of business names that have been covered in earlier sections and is longer than any of the other problems. It serves to evaluate student learning of the indexing rules covered to that point by coding and alphabetizing a list of business names and names of people. Simulated Office Problems permit the students to become acquainted with, and to use, *simulated* filing equipment and materials such as business letters, forms, folders, cabinets, and drawers.

Student motivation is continued at a high level through vocational information that ties in the rules with jobs that require that type of learning.

On completing Book 2, the students will have learned how to index, code, and alphabetize all types of business names and will be prepared for a number of filing jobs now available in the business office.

Simon A. Duncan
Robert A. Schultheis

CONTENTS

FILING BUSINESS NAMES CONTAINING FULL PERSONAL NAMES

In *Book 1, Filing Names of People*, you learned how to file the names of people. Many office jobs require that you also file the names of businesses. For example, the Ames Sports Company sells sports equipment. If you were an invoice clerk for the Ames Sports Company, you would fill out sales invoices like the one below.

AMES SPORTS COMPANY
321 Calvert Avenue
Buffalo, NY 14226-2519

INVOICE

SOLD TO

Sports, Incorporated
14 W. Angel St.
Buffalo, NY 14226-2506

DATE March 3, 19--

OUR ORDER NO. 2016

CUST. ORDER NO. 583

SHIPPED VIA Parker Trucking Co.

TERMS   30 days

QUANTITY	DESCRIPTION	UNIT PRICE		AMOUNT	
1 box	baseballs	81	79	81	79
20	bats	4	29	85	80
	Subtotal			167	59
	Tax			6	70
	Total			174	29

After filling out the sales invoice, you would file it in a folder. You will remember from *Book 1* that a folder has several parts:

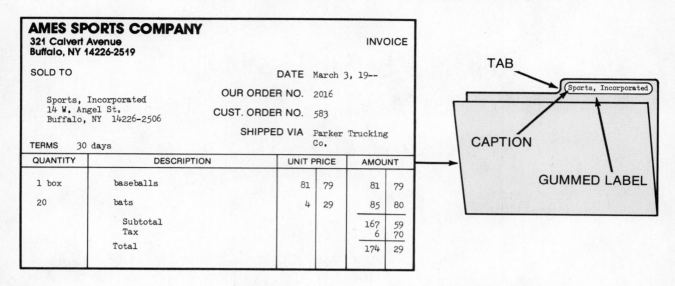

The folder above has a tab that is about half the length of the folder. This is called a ½ cut folder tab. You can buy folders with tabs cut in several ways:

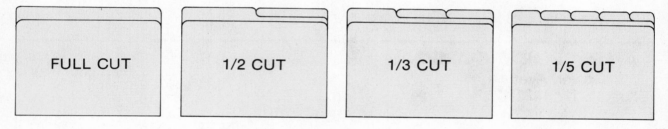

It is important for you to learn how to file business names if you want to get and hold nearly any office job. It is also important for you to learn to use filing supplies and equipment. These are the things you will learn about in the next few pages.

SECTION 1   BUSINESS NAMES WITH FULL PERSONAL NAMES

When you were learning how to file names of people, you learned to follow a simple rule: Arrange names so that the last name is first, the first name or initial is next, and the middle name or initial is last. You will recall that this plan to decide the order in which you would compare names is called *indexing*.

Then, after indexing, compare the names according to the letters of the alphabet until you find a difference. If there is no difference in Unit 1, go to Unit 2 and compare the letters until you come to a difference.

Look at the following two names:

John Schneider
Wilma Weston

The two names are properly indexed below.

Indexing Order

Unit 1	Unit 2
Schneider	John
Weston	Wilma

In the names above, you see a difference in Unit 1 — the first letter of each last name. Because *S* comes before *W* in the alphabet, *Schneider* is arranged before *Weston*.

Alphabetic Order

Schneider, John
Weston, Wilma

If John Schneider is a businessman and owns his own business, he might call his firm *John Schneider Company*.

John Schneider Company

If Wilma Weston also owns a business, she might call her firm *Wilma Weston Agency*.

Wilma Weston Agency

These two *business names containing full personal names* would be indexed and alphabetized in this way:

| Unarranged Names | Indexing Order | | | Alphabetic Order |
	Unit 1	Unit 2	Unit 3	
John Schneider Company	Schneider	John	Company	Schneider, John, Company
Wilma Weston Agency	Weston	Wilma	Agency	Weston, Wilma, Agency

When filing business names you should remember the following:

(1) Business names containing full personal names are indexed so that the last name is the first unit, the first name or initial is the second unit, and the middle name or initial is the third unit.

(2) Certain words like *Company, Incorporated, Corporation, Limited, Agency, Industries*, etc., are used to show that you are dealing with a business name.

(3) *Company, Incorporated, Corporation*, and *Limited* may be abbreviated in the complete business name; but when *indexing* the name, *Co., Inc., Corp.*, and *Ltd*. are always considered to be spelled in full.

(4) The words *Company, Incorporated, Corporation, Limited, Agency, Industries*, etc., are placed after the personal name and become the last indexing unit.

(5) A comma comes before the words *Incorporated* and *Limited* in a business name — for example, Gerard Sherman, Incorporated, and Jonetta Javits, Limited.

(6) A comma separates the personal name from the rest of the business name when the name is put in alphabetic order — for example, Weston, Wilma, Agency.

You are now ready to index and alphabetize business names with full personal names. Notice in the example below that the unarranged names have been indexed and then placed in alphabetic order.

| Unarranged Names | Indexing Order | | | Alphabetic Order |
	Unit 1	Unit 2	Unit 3	
George Richman Co.	Richman	George	Company	Gerard, Sherman, Inc.
Harry Sherman Corp.	Sherman	Harry	Corporation	Richman, George, Co.
Sherman Gerard, Inc.	Gerard	Sherman	Incorporated	Sherman, Harry, Corp.

Practice 1: Index the unarranged names below. Then put them in alphabetic order.

| Unarranged Names | Indexing Order | | | Alphabetic Order |
	Unit 1	Unit 2	Unit 3	
Pearl Malloy Company	_____	_____	_____	_____
Mack Harold Corp.	_____	_____	_____	_____
Jan Belmont Industries	_____	_____	_____	_____
Helene Anderson, Ltd.	_____	_____	_____	_____

As you will recall from your study of personal names, people write their names in many ways. Here are some examples:

Name with full middle name: Julius <u>Harley</u> Stafford

Name with middle initial: Sandra <u>B.</u> Slater

Name with first name as initial:

J. Wallace Tompkins

Name with first and middle
name initials:

B. R. Swift

In each name that has an initial, the initial is used as a separate indexing unit. If the initial is the first name, it becomes Unit 2. If the initial is the middle name, it becomes Unit 3. The last name is always Unit 1.

Any one of these types of names could be used as part of a business name. You will now learn to index and alphabetize business names that contain a person's first name or initial, middle name or initial, and last name.

Notice in the example below that the unarranged names have been indexed and then placed in alphabetic order.

Unarranged Names

1. Julius Harley Stafford Corp.
2. Sandra B. Slater Co.

3. B. R. Swift Agency
4. J. Wallace Tompkins, Inc.

Indexing Order

Unit 1	Unit 2	Unit 3	Unit 4	Alphabetic Order
1. Stafford	Julius	Harley	Corporation	Slater, Sandra B., Co.
2. Slater	Sandra	B.	Company	Stafford, Julius Harley, Corp.
3. Swift	B.	R.	Agency	Swift, B. R., Agency
4. Tompkins	J.	Wallace	Incorporated	Tompkins, J. Wallace, Inc.

Practice 2: Index the unarranged names below. Then put them in alphabetic order.

Unarranged Names

1. Grace Lee Jenkins, Inc.
2. Oscar L. Jenkinson Corp.
3. T. Jane Engel Company

4. T. J. Orlando Corporation
5. Julia R. Otero Co.
6. R. O. English, Inc.

Indexing Order

Unit 1	Unit 2	Unit 3	Unit 4	Alphabetic Order
1. _____	_____	_____	_____	_____
2. _____	_____	_____	_____	_____
3. _____	_____	_____	_____	_____
4. _____	_____	_____	_____	_____
5. _____	_____	_____	_____	_____
6. _____	_____	_____	_____	_____

Notice that the unarranged names below have been indexed. Then they have been placed in alphabetic order in the list of names at the right.

Unarranged Names

1. Will J. Francis, Inc.
2. Frances Williams Company

Indexing Order

Unit 1	Unit 2	Unit 3	Unit 4	Alphabetic Order
1. Francis	Will	J.	Incorporated	
2. Williams	Frances	Company		Francis, W. A., Industries

Francis, W. A., Industries

Francis, Will J., Inc.

Francisco, W. Jaime, Co.

Franciscus, Willi, Corp.

Williams, Frances, Company

Williamson, Arthur, Co.

Practice 3: Index the unarranged names below. Then place them in alphabetic order in the list of names at the right.

Unarranged Names

1. J. J. Nixon Agency
2. Juan J. Miranda Corp.

Indexing Order

Unit 1	Unit 2	Unit 3	Unit 4	Alphabetic Order
1. _____	_____	_____	_____	
2. _____	_____	_____	_____	Michelson, J. J., Ltd.

Michelson, J. J., Ltd.

Moreland, Michelle, Corp.

Nichols, B. B., Inc.

Nicholson, Ruth C., Co.

You will now be asked to put names in folders for a single letter of the alphabet. Notice in the example below that the unarranged names have been indexed. Then a check mark has been placed beside each name to show its correct folder.

		Indexing Order			Folders	
Unarranged Names	**Unit 1**	**Unit 2**	**Unit 3**	**Unit 4**	**C**	**D**
David C. Carroll Agency	Carroll	David	C.	Agency	√	
Judy B. Crawford Co.	Crawford	Judy	B.	Company	√	
Carrie Daniels Corp.	Daniels	Carrie	Corporation			√
D. J. Curran, Inc.	Curran	D.	J.	Incorporated	√	

Practice 4: Index the unarranged names below. Then place a check mark beside each name to show its correct folder.

		Indexing Order			Folders	
Unarranged Names	**Unit 1**	**Unit 2**	**Unit 3**	**Unit 4**	**F**	**G**
Frank G. Glenn Corp.	_____	_____	_____	_____	_____	_____
Gilda D. Frank, Inc.	_____	_____	_____	_____	_____	_____
Gail Fraser Co.	_____	_____	_____	_____	_____	_____
Glen A. Fray Agency	_____	_____	_____	_____	_____	_____
Frank Glass Co.	_____	_____	_____	_____	_____	_____

Notice that the unarranged names below have been indexed. If the indexing order is *correct*, a check mark has been placed under the *Right* column. If the indexing order is *not* correct, a check mark has been placed under the *Wrong* column.

		Indexing Order			Answers	
Unarranged Names	**Unit 1**	**Unit 2**	**Unit 3**	**Unit 4**	**Right**	**Wrong**
Honora Unger Industries	Unger	Honora	Industries		√	
R. Harold Unger Corp.	Unger	Harold	R.	Corporation		√
T. J. Doran Co.	Doran	T.	J.	Company	√	
Myrna Doran Bruce, Inc.	Bruce	Doran	Myrna	Incorporated		√

Practice 5: The unarranged names below have been indexed. If the indexing order is *correct*, place a check mark under the *Right* column. If the indexing order is *not* correct, place a check mark under the *Wrong* column.

		Indexing Order			Answers	
Unarranged Names	**Unit 1**	**Unit 2**	**Unit 3**	**Unit 4**	**Right**	**Wrong**
Sue W. Fleming, Inc.	Fleming	Sue	W.	Incorporated	_____	_____
Sally C. Block Corp.	Block	Sally	C.	Corporation	_____	_____
C. Saul Fleming Co.	Fleming	Saul	C.	Company	_____	_____
Jay Saul Block Co.	Block	Saul	Jay	Company	_____	_____

When you are filing in a business office, you will find that the indexing of names is done in a different way. Instead of writing out the names in indexing order, a number corresponding to the indexing order is placed above *each* part of the company's name. This is called *coding* and looks like this:

Unarranged Names	Alphabetic Order
2 3 1 4 Victor J. Baer, Incorporated	Baer, Victor J., Incorporated
2 3 1 4 J. Victor Baldwin Corporation	Baldwin, J. Victor, Corporation

Integrated Practice A: Code the unarranged names below and then put them in alphabetic order.

Unarranged Names	Alphabetic Order
Victor J. Baer, Incorporated	_____
J. Victor Baldwin Corporation	_____
J. V. Barney Agency	_____
Belle Baldwin, Limited	_____
Belle C. Jacobi Company	_____
B. Barney Justin	_____
H. Fred Jacobi Industries	_____
John C. Barney Agency	_____
Barney C. Jacobi Corporation	_____
John Baer	_____

WHAT HAVE YOU LEARNED IN SECTION 1?

(1) When a person's full name is part of a company name, index the name just as you would index a personal name. The last name is Unit 1, the first name or initial is Unit 2, and the middle name or initial is Unit 3.

(2) Words that show that you are dealing with a business name — Corporation, Incorporated, Company, Agency, Industries, Limited, etc. — are the last indexing unit.

(3) The words Company, Incorporated, Limited, and Corporation may be abbreviated in complete business names; but when indexing the name, Co., Inc., Ltd., and Corp. are always considered to be spelled in full.

(4) A comma comes before the words Incorporated and Limited in a business name.

(5) A comma separates the personal name from the rest of the business name when the name is put in alphabetic order.

(6) In the business office a system of coding is used rather than writing out the names in indexing order.

SECTION 2

COMPLETE INDIVIDUAL NAMES WITH PREFIXES, AND COMPOUND LAST NAMES

In Section 1 you learned that a business name that contains the full name of a person is indexed and alphabetized in the same way as a personal name, and that *Company, Incorporated, Corporation*, etc., becomes the last indexing unit. An example follows.

Unarranged Names

1. Joan P. Jordan
2. Joan P. Jordan Co.

	Indexing Order			Alphabetic Order
Unit 1	**Unit 2**	**Unit 3**	**Unit 4**	
1. Jordan	Joan	P.		Jordan, Joan P.
2. Jordan	Joan	P.	Company	Jordan, Joan P., Co.

You are now ready to work with names with *prefixes* and with compound last names. As you remember, names that have certain letters at the beginning are called *prefixed* names. Here are some names with prefixes:

John De Marco   Rosa De La Palma   William McManus

Henry Di Bella   Phyllis O'Connor   Louis Mac Adams

You have learned that prefixed last names are considered as one name, even though the last name has two parts, both of which may have capital letters. Last names with prefixes are counted as one unit. Here is how the name *Rosa DeLa Palma* would be indexed:

Indexing Order

Unit 1	Unit 2
DeLa Palma	Rosa

The rule remains the same with a business name that contains a prefix. This means that if Phyllis O'Connor started a business and called it Phyllis O'Connor, Inc., you would still consider *O'Connor* as the first indexing unit.

Indexing Order

Unit 1	Unit 2	Unit 3
O'Connor	Phyllis	Incorporated

Notice that the unarranged business names below have been indexed and placed in alphabetic order. You will see that the prefixed last name is the first indexing unit.

Unarranged Names	Indexing Order Unit 1	Unit 2	Unit 3	Alphabetic Order
John DeMarco Corp.	DeMarco	John	Corporation	DeLa Palma, Rosa, Corp.
Henry DiBella, Inc.	DiBella	Henry	Incorporated	DeMarco, John, Corp.
William McManus Co.	McManus	William	Company	DiBella, Henry, Inc.
Rosa DeLa Palma Corp.	DeLa Palma	Rosa	Corporation	McManus, William, Co.
Phyllis O'Connor, Inc.	O'Connor	Phyllis	Incorporated	O'Connor, Phyllis, Inc.

Practice 1: Index the unarranged names below. Then put them in alphabetic order.

Unarranged Names	Indexing Order Unit 1	Unit 2	Unit 3	Alphabetic Order
Louise MacLeod Co.	_____	_____	_____	_____
James O'Donnell Corp.	_____	_____	_____	_____
McGeorge Daniel, Inc.	_____	_____	_____	_____
Antonia DeSena Agency	_____	_____	_____	_____

As you will remember, you learned to index *compound* last names as two units, even though the person with a compound last name thinks of it as one name. An example of such a name is *Anderson-Austin*.

Indexing Order

Unit 1	Unit 2
Anderson-	Austin

A person with a compound last name may go into business and use his or her name for the company name. In this case you would still consider the compound last name as the first *two* indexing units.

Notice in the example below how you would handle compound last names in business names. You will see that the unarranged names have been indexed and then placed in alphabetic order.

Unarranged Names

1. John Elias-Franks Corp.
2. Elsie Irwin-Forbes Company

3. Zack Franks-Martin Industries
4. Ruth Zack-Franks, Incorporated

Indexing Order

Unit 1	Unit 2	Unit 3	Unit 4	Alphabetic Order
1. Elias-	Franks	John	Corporation	Elias-Franks, John, Corp.
2. Irwin-	Forbes	Elsie	Company	Franks-Martin, Zack, Industries
3. Franks-	Martin	Zack	Industries	Irwin-Forbes, Elsie, Company
4. Zack-	Franks	Ruth	Incorporated	Zack-Franks, Ruth, Incorporated

Practice 2: Index the unarranged names below. Then put them in alphabetic order.

Unarranged Names

1. Victor Pagan-Lugo Co.
2. Marie Jeffrey-Jackson Industries

3. Helga Bohn-Burke Agency
4. John DeNicola-Martin Corp.

Indexing Order

Unit 1	Unit 2	Unit 3	Unit 4	Alphabetic Order
1. _____	_____	_____	_____	_____
2. _____	_____	_____	_____	_____
3. _____	_____	_____	_____	_____
4. _____	_____	_____	_____	_____

Notice that the unarranged name below has been coded and placed in alphabetic order in the list of names at the right.

Unarranged Name	Alphabetic Order
3 4 1 2 5	
Viola J. Delgado-Diaz Co.	

Deerfield, Frank J., Corp.

Delgado-Diaz, Viola J., Co.

Della-LaGuardia, R. J., Inc.

DeMeo, Hazel J., Company

Practice 3: Code the unarranged name below and place it in alphabetic order in the list of names at the right.

Unarranged Name   **Alphabetic Order**

Eric C. VanRaalte, Inc.

_____

LeMasters, Ronda, Inc.

_____

VandenPlatt, Lillian, Co.

_____

VonStormer, Heinz, Corp.

_____

Notice that the three unarranged names below have been coded. Then they have been put in alphabetic order in the list of names at the right.

Unarranged Names   **Alphabetic Order**

  2   1   3
1. Ruth deAngelis, Incorporated

de Angelis, Ruth, Incorporated
deStefano, Sal C., Corp.

  3   1   2   4
2. Burt Furman-Danes Company

Furman, Bruce, Inc.
Furman-Danes, Burt, Company
Fusco-Halle, Jon, Industries

  3   1   2   4
3. Kathy Grant-Ford Corporation

Garrett-Daniels, Bill, Company
Grant-Ford, Kathy, Corporation

Practice 4: Code the unarranged names below. Then place them in alphabetic order in the list of names at the right.

Unarranged Names   **Alphabetic Order**

1. J. Davidson-Fromer Agency

_____

Davison-Fromme, John, Corp.

_____

2. Julia Franke-Davidson Corporation

_____

Frost-Martin, Ila, Incorporated

_____

3. Rita Froster-Danton Industries

_____

Froster-Marvin, Helen, Inc.

_____

Frosterman-Davy, Sena, Co.

_____

Notice that the unarranged names below have been coded. However, some of the names are coded incorrectly. These names have been crossed out and coded correctly. Then all the names have been placed in alphabetic order.

Unarranged Names

3   1   2
1. ~~Gerardo deLeon Agency~~
3   1   2   4
2. Henry Demarest-Jonas, Incorporated
3   2   1   4
3. ~~Oscar Delgado-Blanco Company~~
2   1   3
4. Celia George Corporation

Corrected Coding

2   1   3
1. Gerardo deLeon Agency _____

2. _____

3   1   2   4
3. Oscar Delgado-Blanco Company _____

4. _____

Alphabetic Order

deLeon, Gerardo, Agency
Delgado-Blanco, Oscar, Company
Demarest-Jonas, Henry, Incorporated
George, Celia, Corporation

Practice 5: The unarranged names below have been coded. However, some of them are coded incorrectly. Cross out these names and code them correctly in the space provided. Then put all the names in alphabetic order.

Unarranged Names

3   1   2
1. Glenda McClendon, Incorporated
3   1   2   4
2. Calvin Martin-Barnes Corporation
3   1   2
3. Ruth O'Mara Agency
2   1   3
4. Betty VanDrew Company
1   2   3
5. Martin D'Agostino, Incorporated

Corrected Coding

1. _____

2. _____

3. _____

4. _____

5. _____

Alphabetic Order

_____

_____

_____

_____

_____

Integrated Practice B: Code the unarranged names below and then put them in alphabetic order.

Unarranged Names	Alphabetic Order
Julia O'Malley Agency	_____
Stephen Olson-Forde Co.	_____
J. O'Malley Corporation	_____
Oliver Forde Industries	_____
Mollie vonBaum, Inc.	_____
Eric VanDorn, Incorporated	_____
J. VanDorn-Braun Company	_____
J. P. Malley	_____
Oliver Franklin Agency	_____
F. Oliverio, Incorporated	_____
Jane J. Vanderbilt Industries	_____
Josephine Von Baumler, Ltd.	_____

WHAT HAVE YOU LEARNED IN SECTION 2?

(1) If a business name contains a full personal name with a prefixed last name, follow the same rule of indexing as with a personal name: Think of the prefix as part of the last name and use that entire last name as Unit 1.

(2) If a business name contains a full personal name that has a compound last name, think of the compound last name as two names and make them Units 1 and 2.

SECTION 3   COMPLETE INDIVIDUAL NAME WITH KIND OF BUSINESS

Until now you have been working with business names that contain only the name of a person. However, it is very common to have the kind of business included with the name of the person, such as:

George Lincoln <u>Lumber</u> Company

By having the kind of business in the company name, it is easier for people to remember the name when they need the kind of product the company provides.

You now have to decide how to index such a name so that you can put it in correct alphabetic order. As you have always done, use the person's last name as Unit 1, the first name or initial as Unit 2, the middle name or initial as Unit 3, and the type of business as Unit 4. You would index the name above as follows:

George Lincoln Lumber Company

Indexing Order

Unit 1	Unit 2	Unit 3	Unit 4
Lincoln	George	Lumber	Company

If the company name includes a person's middle name or initial, you would follow the usual order of indexing, as follows:

Wendy C. Fuller Deliveries, Incorporated

Indexing Order

Unit 1	Unit 2	Unit 3	Unit 4	Unit 5
Fuller	Wendy	C.	Deliveries	Incorporated

Wendy C. Fuller Deliveries, Incorporated

If the type of business is more than one word, treat each word as a separate unit in the order in which the words appear. Here is an example:

Theodore C. Jenkins Air Freight Co.

Indexing Order

Unit 1	Unit 2	Unit 3	Unit 4	Unit 5	Unit 6
Jenkins	Theodore	C.	Air	Freight	Company

You are now ready to index and alphabetize business names in which the kind of business is used as part of the name. Notice in the example below how the unarranged names have been indexed. Then they have been placed in alphabetic order at the right.

Unarranged Names

1. Paula Spinner Hair Designs
2. Phil Milner Art Studio
3. Paula Stevens Management Co.

Indexing Order

	Unit 1	Unit 2	Unit 3	Unit 4	Alphabetic Order
1.	Spinner	Paula	Hair	Designs	Milner, Phil, Art Studio
2.	Milner	Phil	Art	Studio	Spinner, Paula, Hair Designs
3.	Stevens	Paula	Management	Company	Stevens, Paula, Management Co.

Practice 1: Index the unarranged names below and then place them in alphabetic order.

Unarranged Names

1. Marie Tracey Camera Repair Shop
2. Mark Troy Maid Service
3. J. Torres Designer Suit Factory

Indexing Order

	Unit 1	Unit 2	Unit 3	Unit 4	Unit 5
1.	_____	_____	_____	_____	_____
2.	_____	_____	_____	_____	_____
3.	_____	_____	_____	_____	_____

Alphabetic Order

_____

_____

_____

Notice that the two unarranged names below have been indexed. Then they have been placed in alphabetic order in the list of names at the right.

Unarranged Names

1. Arthur Logan Paints, Inc.
2. Jane Harvey Realty

Indexing Order

Unit 1	Unit 2	Unit 3	Unit 4	Alphabetic Order
1. Logan	Arthur	Paints	Incorporated	*Harvey, Jane, Realty*
				Hoving, George, Books, Inc.
2. Harvey	Jane	Realty		
				Howland, Jessica, Drug Co.
				Logan, Aaron, Meat Packers
				Logan, Arthur, Paints, Inc.
				Love, Alex, Frame Designs

Practice 2: Index the three unarranged names below. Then place them in alphabetic order in the list of names at the right.

Unarranged Names

1. Jill Jaeger Tropical Birds
2. Moses Jenkins Foods Corporation
3. Sy Johnston Designer Fabrics

Indexing Order

Unit 1	Unit 2	Unit 3	Unit 4	Alphabetic Order
1. _____	_____	_____	_____	
				Janeen, J., Coat Co.
2. _____	_____	_____	_____	
				Janeway, Fay, Typing
3. _____	_____	_____	_____	
				Jasper, Ruth, Roofing Co.
				Jimenez, Juan, Mexican Inn

Notice that the unarranged names below have been coded. However, some of the names are coded incorrectly. These names have been crossed out and coded correctly. All the names have then been placed in alphabetic order.

Unarranged Names

1. ~~Lori K. Karp Creations, Incorporated~~
   1 2 3 4 5

2. ~~Carrie Jackson Hardware Company~~
   4 1 2 3

3. Walt Frost Sports, Limited
   2 1 3 4

Corrected Coding

1. Lori K. Karp Creations, Incorporated
   2 3 1 4 5

2. Carrie Jackson Hardware Company
   2 1 3 4

3. _____

Alphabetic Order

Frost, Walt, Sports, Limited

Jackson, Carrie, Hardware Company

Karp, Lori K., Creations, Incorporated

Practice 3: The unarranged names below have been coded. However, some of them are coded incorrectly. Cross out these names and code them correctly. Then put all the names in alphabetic order.

Unarranged Names

1. Lou Nielson Paints
   2 1 3

2. Paul J. Lucas Photo Studio
   1 2 3 4 5

3. Nancy S. Carr Income Tax Service
   2 3 1 4 5 6

4. Jennie Swift Art Supply
   2 1 4 3

Corrected Coding

1. _____

2. _____

3. _____

4. _____

Alphabetic Order

1. _____

2. _____

3. _____

4. _____

The unarranged names below have been coded. However, some of the names have been coded incorrectly. These names have been crossed out and coded correctly. Then all the names have been put in alphabetic order.

Unarranged Names

   2   1   3   4
1. Jay Jordan Photo Company
    1   2   3   4
2. ~~Joyce Jordan Interiors, Incorporated~~
    3   2   4   1
3. ~~Julian Joyce Car Rental~~
    2   1   3   4
4. Jane Joyce Imported Wines

Corrected Coding

1. _____
    2   1   3   4
2. Joyce Jordan Interiors, Incorporated
    2   1   3   4
3. Julian Joyce Car Rental

4. _____

Alphabetic Order

Jordan, Jay, Photo Company

Jordan, Joyce, Interiors, Incorporated

Joyce, Jane, Imported Wines

Joyce, Julian, Car Rental

Practice 4: The unarranged names below have been coded. However, some of the names have been coded incorrectly. Cross out these names and code them correctly. Then put all the names in alphabetic order.

Unarranged Names

   2   1   3
1. Hal Morley Antiques
    2   3   1   4   5
2. Halston T. Morland Publishing Company
    2   3   1   4
3. Morley Halston Shoe Manufacturing
    4   3   2   1
4. M. Halston Creative Designs
    1   2   3   4
5. Helen Morley Computer Store

Corrected Coding

1. _____

2. _____

3. _____

4. _____

5. _____

Alphabetic Order

_____

_____

_____

_____

_____

Code the unarranged names below. Then put them in alphabetic order.

Unarranged Names	Alphabetic Order
Rosa Diaz Travel Agency	_____
Jill Allen Building Contractors	_____
John J. Allan Optical Company	_____
A. P. DuMont Dry Cleaning Co.	_____
Rose Allenby, Inc.	_____
Allen Brooks Bakeries	_____
Seymour Baker Products Co.	_____
Susan P. Allenby Alaskan Furs	_____
P. Baker-Seward Antique Furniture	_____
R. Bakewell Towing Service	_____

WHAT HAVE YOU LEARNED IN SECTION 3?	(1) If a company name contains the full name of a person and the kind of business, index the full name by starting with the person's last name. (2) The kind of business is indexed after the name of the person.

SECTION 4   SIMULATED OFFICE PROBLEMS

Many file drawers contain folders with captions which begin with different letters of the alphabet. To help you file or find a folder with a caption that begins with a certain letter, *file guides* are used. Two kinds of file guides that are often found in offices are shown below.

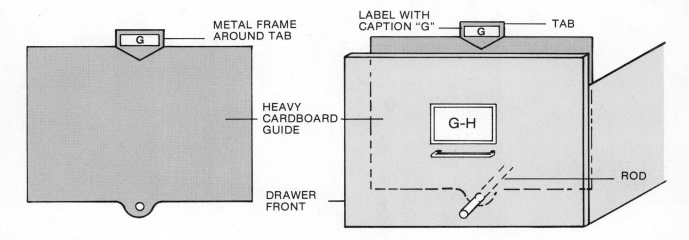

The file guide on the left has the tab strengthened with a metal frame. The file guide on the right does not. Both guides are made of heavy cardboard and have a hole at the bottom through which a rod is passed to hold the guides in place in the file drawer. The rods keep the guides from slipping out of the drawer every time a file folder is removed.

The file drawer below shows how file guides are used to separate folders according to letters of the alphabet.

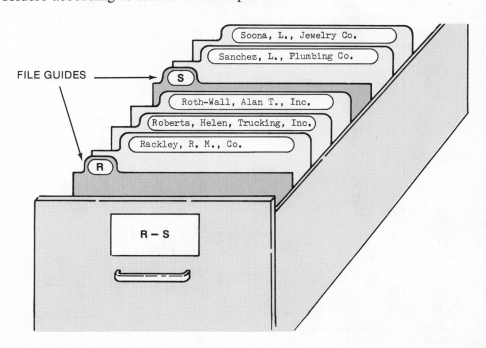

Notice that the unarranged names below have been indexed. Then they have been placed on the folder labels in alphabetic order. A check mark has been placed under the guide behind which each folder should be placed.

Unarranged Names

1. A. Carlos Delmar Machinery
2. R. De Beers Jewelry Co.
3. W. Borg-Alan Industries
4. Grace B. Corleone, Inc.
5. A. L. Chai Moving Co.

Indexing Order

Unit 1	Unit 2	Unit 3	Unit 4	Unit 5
1. Delmar	A.	Carlos	Machinery	
2. De Beers	R.	Jewelry	Company	
3. Borg-	Alan	W.	Industries	
4. Corleone	Grace	B.	Incorporated	
5. Chai	A.	L.	Moving	Company

GUIDES

	A	B	C	D

Delmar, A. Carlos, Machinery ✔ (D)

De Beers, R., Jewelry Company ✔ (D)

Corleone, Grace B., Inc. ✔ (C)

Chai, A. L., Moving Co. ✔ (C)

Borg-Alan, W., Industries ✔ (B)

Practice 1: Index the unarranged names below. Then place them on the folder labels in alphabetic order. Place a check mark under the guide behind which each folder should be filed.

Unarranged Names

1. Harriet L. O'Bannon
2. Julio Minos Travel-Mart
3. H. L. O'Bannon
4. David Nunn-Porter Carpet Co.
5. Harriet L. O'Bannon Realty

Indexing Order

	Unit 1	Unit 2	Unit 3	Unit 4	Unit 5
1.					
2.					
3.					
4.					
5.					

GUIDES

M   N   O   P

When there are many folders which have captions starting with the same letter, you should use extra file guides. These extra guides will help you find and file folders quickly. When you use extra guides, divide a letter into several parts, such as Ea–Ed, Ee–Eh, Ei–El, Em–Ep, Eq–Et, and Eu–Ez.

The file drawer below is divided by file guides which separate the letter *E* into small groups.

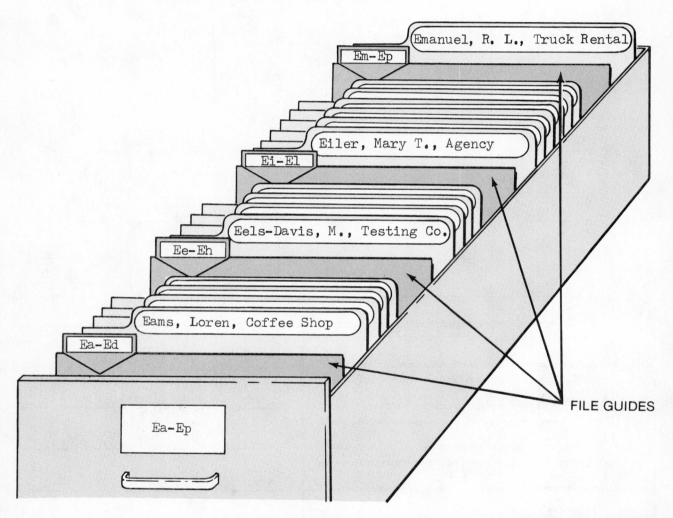

FILE GUIDES

As you can see, file guides help you find any name much faster. The file guides tell you which names are placed in each section of the file drawer.

To Find a Name Quickly, Check the File Guides First.

Notice that the unarranged names below have been indexed. Then they have been placed on the folder labels in alphabetic order. A check mark has been placed under the guide behind which the folder belongs.

Unarranged Names

1. Alan T. Snead
2. L. M. Santoni Drilling Co.
3. L. Bertha Skinner Glass Designers
4. Maria Sola Precious Metals
5. Muhammed Shankar Oil Drilling Co.

Indexing Order

Unit 1	Unit 2	Unit 3	Unit 4	Unit 5
1. Snead	Alan	T.		
2. Santoni	L.	M.	Drilling	Company
3. Skinner	L.	Bertha	Glass	Designers
4. Sola	Maria	Precious	Metals	
5. Shankar	Muhammed	Oil	Drilling	Company

GUIDES

Sa–Sd   Se–Sh   Si–Sl   Sm–Sp

Sola, Maria, Precious Metals ✔ (Sm–Sp)

Snead, Alan T. ✔ (Sm–Sp)

Skinner, L. Bertha, Glass Designers ✔ (Si–Sl)

Shankar, Muhammed, Oil Drilling Co. ✔ (Se–Sh)

Santoni, L. M., Drilling Co. ✔ (Sa–Sd)

Practice 2: Index the unarranged names below. Then place them on the folder labels in alphabetic order. Place a check mark under the guide behind which the folder belongs.

Unarranged Names

1. Anton London Floral Arrangements
2. T. N. La Mar Tool Manufacturing
3. Miguel R. Lucia-Lancia
4. T. N. Lamar Tools, Ltd.
5. Bonnie Lindsay Cab Company

Indexing Order

	Unit 1	Unit 2	Unit 3	Unit 4	Unit 5
1.	_____	_____	_____	_____	_____
2.	_____	_____	_____	_____	_____
3.	_____	_____	_____	_____	_____
4.	_____	_____	_____	_____	_____
5.	_____	_____	_____	_____	_____

GUIDES

La-Le   Lf-Lj   Lk-Lo   Lp-Lu

Notice that *two* of the folders in the file drawer below were filed behind the *wrong* guide. The names on the two incorrectly filed folders have been written on the lines at the right. Then a check mark has been placed under the file guide behind which each of the folders should have been placed.

GUIDES

INCORRECTLY FILED FOLDERS   Ca-Ce   Cf-Cj

Cicero, Elisa _____ _____ ✓
Cella, Clara, Printing Plant ✓ _____

Practice 3: Find *two* folders which were filed behind the *wrong* guide. Then write the names on the lines at the right. Place a check mark under the file guide behind which each of the folders should have been placed.

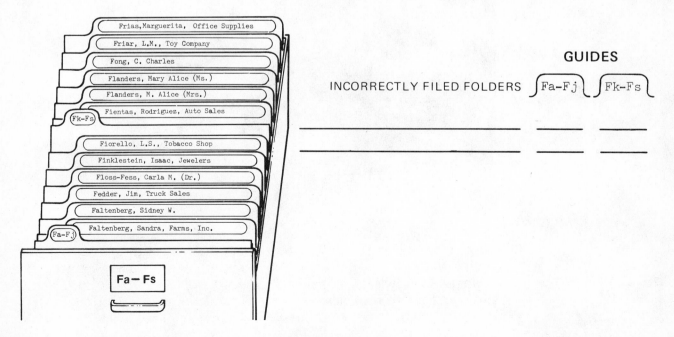

GUIDES

INCORRECTLY FILED FOLDERS   Fa-Fj   Fk-Fs

_____ _____ _____
_____ _____ _____

Guides are also used in sorters. Sorters are used to sort a large number of cards, letters, folders, or other items which you are going to file so that your filing becomes easier. The sorter has a section for each letter of the alphabet. Some sorters group several letters of the alphabet into one section.

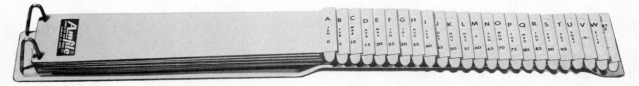

Desk Top Sorter

Boorum & Pease Co.

Large Round Sorter

Photo courtesy of TAB Products Co.

For example, if you had 50 folders to file in a large filing department, it would be easier for you to sort the folders into groups (A–E, F–J, K–O, P–T, U–Z) before you begin to put the folders into the file cabinets. Otherwise, you might file the first folder you pick up under *B* and then have to walk across the room to file the next folder under *T*. A sorter helps you avoid crisscrossing the room and speeds up your filing.

The folders below need to be sorted before they are filed. A check mark has been placed below the sorter guide behind which each folder should be placed.

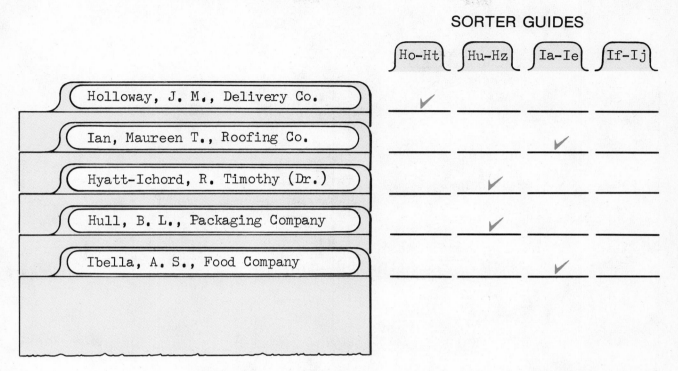

SORTER GUIDES

Ho-Ht	Hu-Hz	Ia-Ie	If-Ij
Holloway, J. M., Delivery Co. ✔			
Ian, Maureen T., Roofing Co.		✔	
Hyatt-Ichord, R. Timothy (Dr.)	✔		
Hull, B. L., Packaging Company	✔		
Ibella, A. S., Food Company		✔	

Practice 4: The folders below need to be sorted before they are filed. Place a check mark below the sorter guide behind which each folder should be placed.

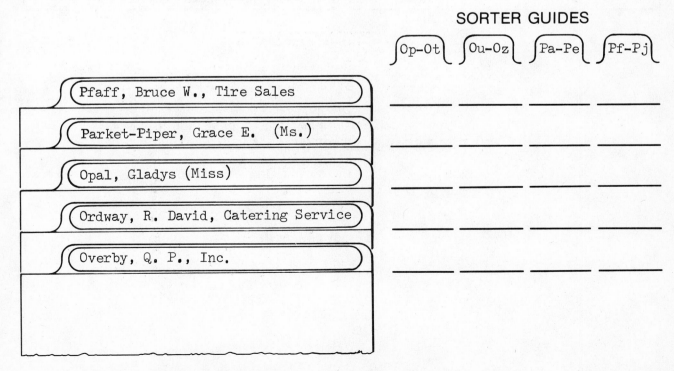

SORTER GUIDES

Op-Ot	Ou-Oz	Pa-Pe	Pf-Pj
Pfaff, Bruce W., Tire Sales			
Parket-Piper, Grace E. (Ms.)			
Opal, Gladys (Miss)			
Ordway, R. David, Catering Service			
Overby, Q. P., Inc.			

In an office, you usually index the names of persons and businesses on the letters or papers to be filed. For example:

```
┌─────────────────────────────────┐   ┌─────────────────────────────────────┐
│            OFFICE COPY          │   │                            INVOICE   │
│                                 │   │                                      │
│  January 1, 19--                │   │  AUSTIN LUMBER SUPPLY                 │
│     2    1    3    4            │   │  1700 North Boulevard                 │
│  Mildred Turney Sports Company  │   │  Austin, TX  78746-4321              │
│  415 North Main Street          │   │  CUSTOMER ORDER NO. 4003 DATE April 20 19 -- │
│  Hayward, CA  94546-7102        │   │       2    3    1    4    5          │
│                                 │   │  NAME   J. J. Beard Lumber Co.       │
│  Gentlemen                      │   │  ADDRESS   618 Amarillo St.          │
│                                 │   │  Austin, TX  78746-1637              │
│  Please deliver 1200 Tennis Kits│   │                                      │
│  to our branch warehouse on     │   │  QUANTITY │ DESCRIPTION │PRICE│AMOUNT │
│  Carlton Street as soon as      │   │   200    │4X8 Plywood │$12.00│$2,400.00│
│  possible.                      │   │          │ SALES TAX  │ 4%  │  96.00 │
│                                 │   │          │ TOTAL      │     │$2,496.00│
│  Sincerely Yours                │   │                                      │
│                                 │   │                                      │
│  Allen Bates                    │   │                                      │
│  Purchasing Manager             │   │  RECEIVED BY   RMD                    │
└─────────────────────────────────┘   └─────────────────────────────────────┘
```

When you index on the business paper itself, it is called *coding*. When you code, you *number* the indexing units in correct indexing order. In most offices, coding is done with a colored pen or pencil.

When you look at the coded letter above, you know that the correct indexing order is:

Turney, Mildred, Sports Company

When you look at the invoice above, you know that the correct indexing order is:

Beard, J. J., Lumber Co.

Part 1 • Filing Business Names Containing Full Personal Names

The names on the letters below have been coded. Notice that each indexing unit has been numbered in correct indexing order.

```
May 24, 19--

 3   1   2       4
W. Gant-Prell, Incorporated
89 Pier Street
Roanoke, VA   24012-7310
```

```
May 12, 19--

 2    3   1    4
Thomas H. Hart Company
9900 Federal Drive
Takoma, WA   98499-3920
```

```
May 2, 19--

 2   3   1    4   5
N. Nancy Kregel Storage Co.
509 Torrance Avenue
Charleston, SC   29405-3219
```

```
May 9, 19--

 2   3   1    4        5
G. P. Hanley Products, Inc.
10 North Stevenson Street
Stillwater, OK   74074-9971
```

Practice 5: Code the names on the letters below by numbering each indexing unit in correct indexing order.

```
May 1, 19--


J. B. LaBell Company
112 Anderson Street
Biloxi, MS   39531-5689
```

```
May 2, 19--


Ralston P. Wisinski Appliances
Grandview Drive
Sante Fe, NM   87502-9002
```

```
October 23, 19--


Marianne Cross Lighting Store
45 Industrial Road
Topeka, KS   66608-4276
```

```
January 16, 19--


T. Thomas O'Donnell Agency
9000 Overbrook Lane
New Haven, CT   06513-3112
```

```
June 5, 19--


Patricia Minosa Plumbing Company
13 East Avenue
Baton Rouge, LA   70802-5190
```

```
March 3, 19--


K. Talbot Stone Industries
24 Longpoint Road
Boise, ID   83704-8944
```

```
November 28, 19--


Karen Kraft Interior Designs
9870 Seaview Lane
Honolulu, HI   96815-4930
```

```
February 4, 19--


W. Koper-Winn Molding Co.
8977 Bartels Avenue
Newark, NJ   07105-7323
```

Now you will learn to code and then file letters in folders. Notice that the names on the letters below have been coded by numbering the indexing units. Then the letters have been filed in one of the two folders by writing the folder number beside each letter.

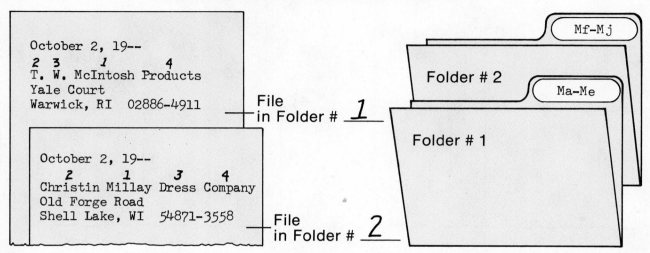

October 2, 19--
 2 3   1   4
T. W. McIntosh Products
Yale Court
Warwick, RI   02886-4911

File in Folder # *1*

October 2, 19--
        2   1   3   4
Christin Millay Dress Company
Old Forge Road
Shell Lake, WI   54871-3558

File in Folder # *2*

Folder # 2
Folder # 1
Mf-Mj
Ma-Me

Practice 6: File the letters below by coding each letter and then writing the correct folder number on the line beside each letter.

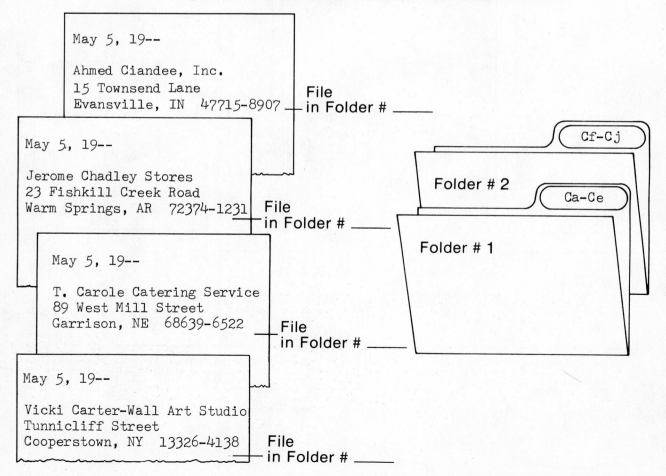

May 5, 19--

Ahmed Ciandee, Inc.
15 Townsend Lane
Evansville, IN   47715-8907

File in Folder # _____

May 5, 19--

Jerome Chadley Stores
23 Fishkill Creek Road
Warm Springs, AR   72374-1231

File in Folder # _____

May 5, 19--

T. Carole Catering Service
89 West Mill Street
Garrison, NE   68639-6522

File in Folder # _____

May 5, 19--

Vicki Carter-Wall Art Studio
Tunnicliff Street
Cooperstown, NY   13326-4138

File in Folder # _____

Folder # 2
Folder # 1
Cf-Cj
Ca-Ce

2

FILING BUSINESS NAMES WITH DESCRIPTIVE WORDS OR PERSONAL NAMES

So far you have learned how to file the names of businesses that have the full name of a person in the title or that have the person's name and the type of business in the title. For example:

Jonice Wilson, Inc.
Jonice Wilson Trucking Company

However, many businesses have names like these:

American Foundry Corporation
Barnum-Bailey Circus
LeMay Ferry Stores, Inc.

You have also learned that file folders are cut with tabs in many positions. For example:

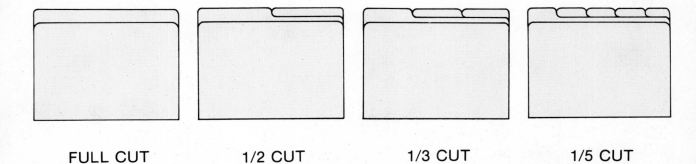

FULL CUT   1/2 CUT   1/3 CUT   1/5 CUT

The different tab cuts are used to make filing and finding folders in a file drawer easier. For example, look at the file drawer on page 34.

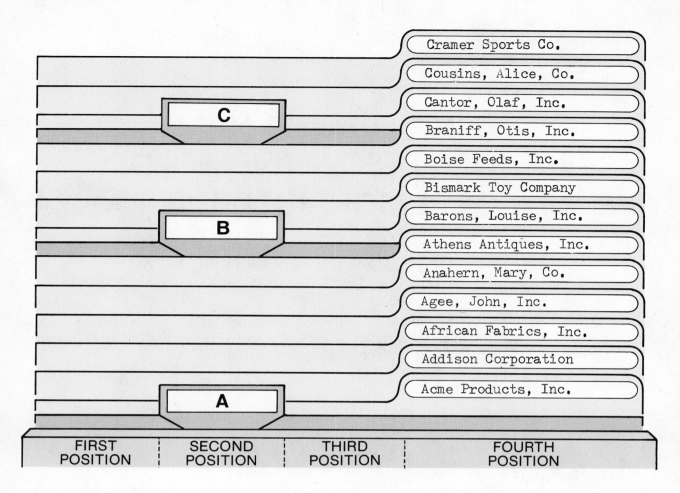

Notice that the file drawer has been divided into *positions*. The file guides are in the second position and the folder tabs are in the fourth position. You can see that putting all guides in the second position and all folder tabs in the fourth position makes it very easy to see how the file drawer is organized.

In Part 2 you will learn how to:

1. File business names like American Foundry Corporation.
2. Use different size tab cuts.
3. Decide what to place in each file drawer position.

SECTION 1   BUSINESS NAMES THAT INCLUDE ONLY PART OF A
PERSON'S NAME

You have been working with business names that include the full
name of a person. As long as a business name includes a full personal
name, index according to the rules for full personal names. This means
that the last name comes first as Unit 1. The first name is Unit 2, and
any middle name or initial is Unit 3.

It is very common to see business names that include only the first
or last name of a person. Here is an example:

Wilson Tool Corp.

This type of business name is very easy to index: Index the name in
the order in which it is written. Each part of the name is a separate
unit. This is how you would index *Wilson Tool Corp.*:

Indexing Order

Unit 1	Unit 2	Unit 3
Wilson	Tool	Corporation

As is true in the example above, the company name may contain
words that describe the kind of business it is. If the name does include
such descriptive words, arrange the words in the order in which they
appear.

Notice how the unarranged names below have been indexed and placed in alphabetic order.

Unarranged Names

1. Williams Fine Fruit Company
2. Blanco Repair Service
3. Jennings Book Corp.
4. Wright Electric Co.
5. Yates Garden Mart

Indexing Order

Unit 1	Unit 2	Unit 3	Unit 4	Alphabetic Order
1. Williams	Fine	Fruit	Company	Blanco Repair Service
2. Blanco	Repair	Service		Jennings Book Corp.
3. Jennings	Book	Corporation		Williams Fine Fruit Company
4. Wright	Electric	Company		Wright Electric Co.
5. Yates	Garden	Mart		Yates Garden Mart

Practice 1: Index the unarranged names below. Then put them in alphabetic order.

Unarranged Names

1. Cortes Auto Repairs, Inc.
2. Bailey Jewelers, Inc.
3. Cuevas Candy Co.
4. Brandon Fine Jewelers Co.
5. Carey Flower Arrangements

Indexing Order

Unit 1	Unit 2	Unit 3	Unit 4	Alphabetic Order
1. _____	_____	_____	_____	_____
2. _____	_____	_____	_____	_____
3. _____	_____	_____	_____	_____
4. _____	_____	_____	_____	_____
5. _____	_____	_____	_____	_____

You are now ready to place *two* names into a list of names that is already in alphabetic order. Notice that the unarranged names below have been indexed and placed in alphabetic order in the list of names at the right.

Unarranged Names

1. Wriston Hair Cremes, Inc.
2. Tully Auto Cleaners Co.

Indexing Order

Unit 1	Unit 2	Unit 3	Unit 4	Alphabetic Order
1. Wriston	Hair	Cremes	Incorporated	
				Stringly Drugs, Inc.
2. Tully	Auto	Cleaners	Company	
				Tackman Cleaners Co.
				Thompson Deliveries, Inc.
				Tully Auto Cleaners Co.
				Winchell Fruit Co.
				Wriston Hair Cremes, Inc.

Practice 2: Index the unarranged names below. Then put them in alphabetic order.

Unarranged Names

1. Allison Shoe Repair
2. Bromley Shoes, Inc.

Indexing Order

Unit 1	Unit 2	Unit 3	Unit 4	Alphabetic Order
1. _____	_____	_____	_____	
				Albert Fur Styles, Inc.
2. _____	_____	_____	_____	
				Albertson Auto Parts Outlet
				Barlow Books, Inc.
				Bates Super Service Corp.

The unarranged names below have been indexed. If the indexing order is *correct*, a check mark has been placed in the *Right* column. If the indexing order is *not* correct, a check mark has been placed in the *Wrong* column.

| Unarranged Names | Indexing Order | | | | Answers | |
	Unit 1	Unit 2	Unit 3	Unit 4	Right	Wrong
Freeman Sign Repairs Co.	Freeman	Sign	Repairs	Company	✓	
Arnold Bake Shops	Arnold	Shops	Bake			✓
Norwood Fine Bakery	Fine	Norwood	Bakery			✓

Practice 3: If the indexing order for the names below is *correct*, place a check mark in the *Right* column. If the indexing order is *not* correct, place a check mark in the *Wrong* column.

| Unarranged Names | Indexing Order | | | Answers | |
	Unit 1	Unit 2	Unit 3	Right	Wrong
Unger Print Shops	Unger	Print	Shops		
Price Paint Stores	Price	Stores	Paint		
Carmichael Quality Storage	Carmichael	Storage	Quality		

The unarranged names below have been coded and placed in alphabetic order.

Unarranged Names	Alphabetic Order
1. Halsey Auto Parts, Inc. 1 2 3 4	Buford Food Corp.
2. Buford Food Corp. 1 2 3	Halsey Auto Parts, Inc.
3. Lugo Carpet Company 1 2 3	Halstead Master Bakers, Inc.
4. Halstead Master Bakers, Inc. 1 2 3 4	Lugo Carpet Company

Practice 4: Code the list of unarranged names below and then place them in alphabetic order.

Unarranged Names	Alphabetic Order
1. Brill Fine Fur Salon	_____
2. Prince Window Cleaning Co.	_____
3. Allwood Bicycle Shop	_____
4. Cartwright Toy Corp.	_____
5. Serrano Tile Floors, Inc.	_____
6. Thompson Heating Corp.	_____

Part 2 • Filing Business Names with Descriptive Words or Personal Names

The names below have been coded. If the coding is *correct*, a check mark has been placed in the *Right* column. If the coding is *not* correct, a check mark has been placed in the *Wrong* column.

Coded Names	Answers	
	Right	**Wrong**
1 2 3 1. Kober Food Market	✓	
1 3 4 2 2. Wilder Sports Shops, Inc.		✓
1 2 3 4 3. Harwood Hair Styles, Inc.	✓	
1 3 2 4. Haynes Hardware Company		✓
1 2 3 5. Jiminez Bakery Products	✓	

Practice 5: The names below have been coded. If the coding is *correct*, place a check mark in the *Right* column. If the coding is *not* correct, place a check mark in the *Wrong* column.

Coded Names	Answers	
	Right	**Wrong**
1 2 3 1. Allison Catering Service	1. _____	_____
1 3 2 2. Twining Bicycle Shop	2. _____	_____
1 2 3 3. Lyman Shirt Store	3. _____	_____
1 2 4 3 4. Winfield Dairy Foods, Inc.	4. _____	_____
1 2 3 5. Hernandez Vending Machines	5. _____	_____
2 1 4 3 6. Lin Shoe Repair Shops	6. _____	_____
2 1 3 7. Vegas Printing, Inc.	7. _____	_____
1 2 3 8. Herman Cheese Store	8. _____	_____

Integrated Practice D: Code the unarranged names below and then put them in alphabetic order.

Unarranged Names

1. Eastman Fashions Corp.
2. Grace J. Eastman Designers
3. Jerry Erwin Pest Control
4. J. Erwin Flowers
5. Sal Rossi-Gerard Coats, Inc.

6. Eastman Fashions Co.
7. Pride Car Rental
8. Serrano Moving Company
9. Serrano Glove Corp.
10. Gerard Boat Cleaners

Alphabetic Order

1. _____
2. _____
3. _____
4. _____
5. _____
6. _____
7. _____
8. _____
9. _____
10. _____

WHAT HAVE YOU LEARNED IN SECTION 1?

(1) When a business name consists of only the first or last name of a person and a description of the business, index the name in the order in which it is written.
(2) Each part of such a business name is a separate indexing unit.

SECTION 2   BUSINESS NAMES WITHOUT A PERSON'S NAME

As you know, a business name does not have to include a person's name. Some of the biggest and best-known companies use such words as *American, United, National*, and so forth. Here are some examples:

American Broadcasting Co.
United Artists Corp.
National Car Rental System

The order in which you index these names follows the order in which the company name is written. This is how the names shown above would be indexed:

Indexing Order

Unit 1	Unit 2	Unit 3	Unit 4
American	Broadcasting	Company	
United	Artists	Corporation	
National	Car	Rental	System

You are now ready to index and alphabetize business names that don't include a person's name. The unarranged names below have been indexed and then placed in alphabetic order.

Unarranged Names

1. Highway Auto Repairs, Inc.
2. Boulevard Restaurant
3. County Insurance Co.
4. Borough Dry Cleaners

	Unit 1	Unit 2	Unit 3	Unit 4	Alphabetic Order
	Indexing Order				
1.	Highway	Auto	Repairs	Incorporated	Borough Dry Cleaners
2.	Boulevard	Restaurant			Boulevard Restaurant
3.	County	Insurance	Company		County Insurance Co.
4.	Borough	Dry	Cleaners		Highway Auto Repairs, Inc.

Practice 1: Index the unarranged names below. Then put them in alphabetic order.

Unarranged Names

1. Holiday Vacation Time Co.
2. Eastern Air Freight
3. Premier Cosmetics Corp.
4. United Metal Products

Indexing Order

	Unit 1	Unit 2	Unit 3	Unit 4	Alphabetic Order
1.	_____	_____	_____	_____	_____
2.	_____	_____	_____	_____	_____
3.	_____	_____	_____	_____	_____
4.	_____	_____	_____	_____	_____

The unarranged names below have been indexed and then placed in alphabetic order.

Unarranged Names

1. Standard Kitchen Tables Co.
2. Roadside Fresh Fruit

Indexing Order

	Unit 1	Unit 2	Unit 3	Unit 4	Alphabetic Order
1.	Standard	Kitchen	Tables	Company	Realty Insurers, Inc.
					Roadside Fresh Fruit
2.	Roadside	Fresh	Fruit		Standard Carpeting Co.
					Standard Kitchen Tables Co.
					Triangle Building Repairs, Inc.
					Whistlestop Restaurant

Practice 2: Index the unarranged names below and then place them in alphabetic order.

Unarranged Names

1. Equitable Credit Corp.
2. Modern Janitorial Service

	Indexing Order			**Alphabetic Order**
	Unit 1	**Unit 2**	**Unit 3**	
1.	_____	_____	_____	
				Enterprise Investment Corp.
2.	_____	_____	_____	
				Mixing Equipment Co.
				Modern Store Fixtures Co.
				Variety Flower Co.
				_____

The unarranged names below have been indexed. Then a check mark was placed by each name to show the folder in which it should be placed.

		Indexing Order		**Folders**	
Unarranged Names	**Unit 1**	**Unit 2**	**Unit 3**	**H**	**I**
International Meat Markets	International	Meat	Markets		✓
Health Food Imports	Health	Food	Imports	✓	
Investor Loan Corp.	Investor	Loan	Corporation		✓

Practice 3: Index the unarranged names below. Then place a check mark beside each name to show the folder in which it should be placed.

		Indexing Order		**Folders**	
Unarranged Names	**Unit 1**	**Unit 2**	**Unit 3**	**J**	**K**
Jet Machine Co.	_____	_____	_____	___	___
Keyboard Music Co.	_____	_____	_____	___	___
Jamboree Sports Shop	_____	_____	_____	___	___

The unarranged names below have been coded and placed in alphabetic order.

Unarranged Names	Alphabetic Order
1 2 3 4	Alliance Hand Tools Factory
Allied Window Glass Industries	Allied Chemical Corp.
1 2 3 4	Allied Wallpaper, Inc.
Alliance Hand Tools Factory	Allied Window Glass Industries
1 2 3 4	Alpine Vacation Tours, Inc.
Alpine Vacation Tours, Inc.	
1 2 3	
Allied Wallpaper, Inc.	
1 2 3	
Allied Chemical Corp.	

Practice 4: Code the unarranged names below. Then place them in alphabetic order.

Unarranged Names	Alphabetic Order
General Auto Supplies	_____
American Alarm Company	_____
Amity Insurance Agency	_____
Galaxy Cocktails	_____
Furniture Fashions, Inc.	_____
Glass Creations	_____

Integrated Practice E: Code the unarranged names below and then put them in alphabetic order.

Unarranged Names	Alphabetic Order
Globe Paper Products, Inc.	_____
Ideal Printers, Inc.	_____
Liberty Print Shops	_____
Planned Social Research Corp.	_____
Public Book Printing Co.	_____
Ideal Painters Corp.	_____
Frank Glober Printing Co.	_____
Herbert J. Globe-White	_____

WHAT HAVE YOU LEARNED IN SECTION 2?	(1) When a business name does not include the name of a person, index the name in the order in which it is written. (2) Each part of the name is a separate indexing unit.

SECTION 3   COMPOUND BUSINESS NAMES

You have already learned how to handle compound personal last names. As you remember, these are two names joined together by a hyphen to make one name. To make it easier to file, think of such names as two different names, even though they make up the last name of only one person. Here are some examples of the way you handled compound last names:

		Indexing Order		
Unarranged Names	Unit 1	Unit 2	Unit 3	Unit 4
Julia Steiner-Grant	Steiner-	Grant	Julia	
R. J. Martin-Hoover	Martin-	Hoover	R.	J.

In the business world, it is very common for two people to form a company and to use both of their names in the company name. For example, you might find that James Wilson and Rochelle Howell went into business together and used both of their names in the company name. The name of their company might be:

Wilson-Howell Products, Inc.

When you index a compound business name, follow the same rule you learned in indexing a compound personal last name: Treat each of the names as a separate indexing unit. This is the way you would index Wilson-Howell Products, Inc.:

	Indexing Order		
Unit 1	Unit 2	Unit 3	Unit 4
Wilson-	Howell	Products	Incorporated

You are now ready to index and alphabetize compound business names. Notice that the unarranged names below were indexed and then put in alphabetic order.

Unarranged Names

1. Mullins-Hauser Glove Co.
2. Frostman-Jamison Stores Corp.
3. Buttman-Haley Computer Store
4. Armando-Troiano Electric Co.
5. Nader-Holt Costumes

Indexing Order

Unit 1	Unit 2	Unit 3	Unit 4	Alphabetic Order
1. Mullins-	Hauser	Glove	Company	Armando-Troiano Electric Co.
2. Frostman-	Jamison	Stores	Corporation	Buttman-Haley Computer Store
3. Buttman-	Haley	Computer	Store	Frostman-Jamison Stores Corp.
4. Armando-	Troiano	Electric	Company	Mullins-Hauser Glove Co.
5. Nader-	Holt	Costumes		Nader-Holt Costumes

Practice 1: Index the unarranged names below and then put them in alphabetic order.

Unarranged Names

1. Amster-Bellman Travel Co.
2. Bergman-Dunne Cleaners
3. Grimes-Langly Advertising Co.
4. Stokely-Gray Fuel Co.
5. Lindsay-Harmon, Inc.
6. Hoover-Moses Antiques

Indexing Order

Unit 1	Unit 2	Unit 3	Unit 4	Alphabetic Order
1. _____	_____	_____	_____	_____
2. _____	_____	_____	_____	_____
3. _____	_____	_____	_____	_____
4. _____	_____	_____	_____	_____
5. _____	_____	_____	_____	_____
6. _____	_____	_____	_____	_____

The unarranged names below have been indexed. Then they have been placed in alphabetic order in the list of names at the right.

Unarranged Names

1. Tully-Hellman Beverage Corp.
2. Hellman-Tudor Carpet Co.

Indexing Order

Unit 1	Unit 2	Unit 3	Unit 4	Alphabetic Order
1. Tully-	Hellman	Beverage	Corporation	
				Halsten Data Processing
2. Hellman-	Tudor	Carpet	Company	*Hellman-Tudor Carpet Co.*
				Hellman-Turner Exports
				Temple-Hyman Motor Co.
				Temple Lawn Service
				Tully-Hellman Beverage Corp.

Practice 2: Index the unarranged names below and then place them in alphabetic order in the list at the right.

Unarranged Names

1. Milner-Thornton Glass Co.
2. Harwood-Packer Real Estate

Indexing Order

	Unit 1	Unit 2	Unit 3	Unit 4	Alphabetic Order
1.	_____	_____	_____	_____	
					Hanson-Delaney Pharmacy
2.	_____	_____	_____	_____	
					Harvey-Beck Country Estates
					Miller Lampshades Corp.
					Milston-Treat Mattress Co.
					Milstone Natural Foods Corp.

The unarranged names below have been indexed. If the indexing order is *correct*, a check mark has been placed in the *Right* column. If the indexing order is *not* correct, a check mark has been placed in the *Wrong* column.

Unarranged Names

1. Sterling-Carter Paints
2. Allison-Beamis Shirt Co.
3. Cutler-Stone Ovens, Inc.
4. Allison-Baumler Pastries Co.

	Indexing Order			Answers	
Unit 1	**Unit 2**	**Unit 3**	**Unit 4**	**Right**	**Wrong**
1. Sterling-	Carter	Paints		✓	
2. Allison-	Beamis	Shirt	Company	✓	
3. Cutler-	Stone	Ovens	Incorporated	✓	
4. Allison-	Baumler	Company	Pastries		✓

Practice 3: If the indexing order in the following names is *correct*, place a check mark in the *Right* column. If the indexing order is *not* correct, place a check mark in the *Wrong* column.

Unarranged Names

1. Arkin-Regal Mufflers, Inc.
2. Frank Arkin-Regal, Inc.
3. Cranford-Fowler Home Designers
4. Rhonda-Robertson Neckwear Corp.

	Indexing Order			Answers	
Unit 1	**Unit 2**	**Unit 3**	**Unit 4**	**Right**	**Wrong**
1. Arkin-	Regal	Mufflers	Incorporated		
2. Arkin-	Regal	Frank	Incorporated		
3. Cranford-	Home	Fowler	Designers		
4. Rhonda-	Robertson	Neckwear	Corporation		

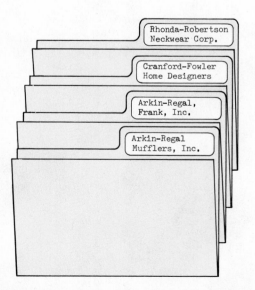

Part 2   •   Filing Business Names with Descriptive Words or Personal Names

The unarranged names below have been coded and placed in alphabetic order.

Unarranged Names

  1   2   3   4
Peters-Selwyn Construction Co.
2 3   1   4
J. C. Peterson Corporation
   1   2   3   4
Peters-Selmon Photographic Supplies
     1   2   3   4
Superior Heating Oil Corp.
    1   2   3   4
Talbert-Gillian Fun Deck

Alphabetic Order

Peters-Selmon Photographic Supplies
Peters-Selwyn Construction Co.
Peterson, J. C., Corporation
Superior Heating Oil Corp.
Talbert-Gillian Fun Deck

Practice 4: Code the unarranged names below and then place them in alphabetic order.

Unarranged Names

Frostman-Farley Leather Co.

Farley-Freed Transport Co.

Davis-Freed Discount Stores

Frostman Laundry Supplies, Inc.

Freed-Langley Paper Co.

David Pope Funeral Home

Alphabetic Order

_____

_____

_____

_____

_____

_____

The names below have been coded. If the coding is *correct*, a check mark has been placed in the *Right* column. If the coding is *not* correct, a check mark has been placed in the *Wrong* column.

	Answers	
Coded Names	**Right**	**Wrong**
3 4 1 2 Harrison-Day Discount Center		✓
1 2 3 4 Grant-Harris Camera Repair	✓	
1 2 3 4 Harvey-Martin Auto Dealership	✓	
2 1 3 4 Harman-Gray Publishing Company		✓
1 2 3 4 Haines-Simons Stationery Co.	✓	

Practice 5: Look at each coded name in the list below. If the name has been coded *correctly*, place a check mark in the *Right* column. If the name has *not* been coded correctly, place a check mark in the *Wrong* column.

	Answers	
Coded Names	**Right**	**Wrong**

2 1 3
Stewart-Reiley Photography   1. _____ _____

1 2 3
Steed-Hammond Architects   2. _____ _____

1 2 3
Stallsmith-Fernandez Garage   3. _____ _____

2 3 1 4
Snook-Veith Lumber Co.   4. _____ _____

Integrated Practice F: Code the unarranged names below and then put them in alphabetic order.

Unarranged Names	**Alphabetic Order**
Carrol-Foster Luggage Co.	_____
William J. Carroll, Inc.	_____
Wilson-Foster Manufacturing	_____
J. Forester Picture Framers	_____
Forrester Typewriter Repair	_____
Forester-Hilton Markets Co.	_____
Forrester Solar Heating, Inc.	_____
Henry J. Foster Company	_____
J. Fosterman Foods, Inc.	_____
L. Carrol-Hinton Clocks, Inc.	_____
Caster Bus Service, Inc.	_____
Harrison-Caster Home Deliveries	_____

WHAT HAVE YOU LEARNED IN SECTION 3?

(1) Compound business names may stand for either one or two persons.
(2) Always consider compound business names as two units. The first name will be Unit 1, and the second name will be Unit 2.

Part 2 • Filing Business Names with Descriptive Words or Personal Names

SECTION 4

SIMULATED OFFICE PROBLEMS

If you worked as a records clerk in a sales office, you probably would have to file folders for customers. Notice that the unarranged customer names below have been coded. Then they have been printed in alphabetic order on file folder labels and the folders have been placed in the fourth position in the drawer.

Unarranged Customer Names

   1   2   3
National Auto Parts

   1   2   3
Maria Nealy, Inc.

   1   2   3
Newark Transit Company

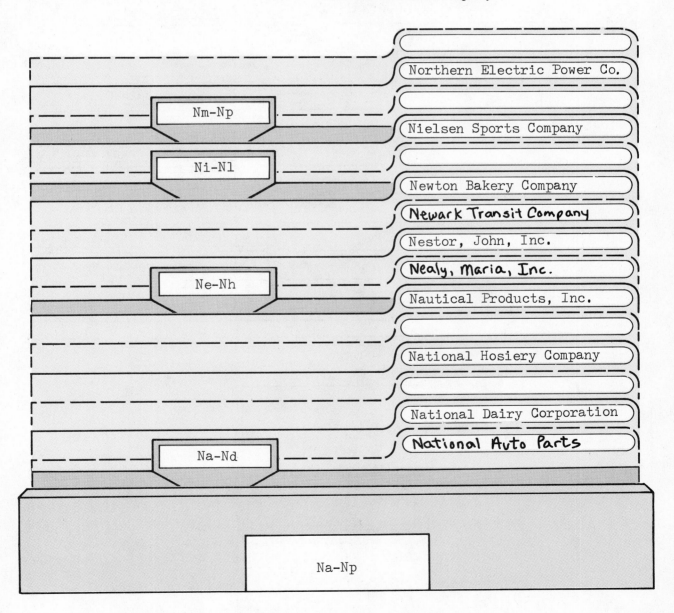

Practice 1: Code the unarranged customer names below. Then print them in alphabetic order on the blank file folder labels provided.

Unarranged Customer Names

Kirsten Vic Allen, Inc.

Vladimer Vending Machines, Inc.

Vickery Fashions Company

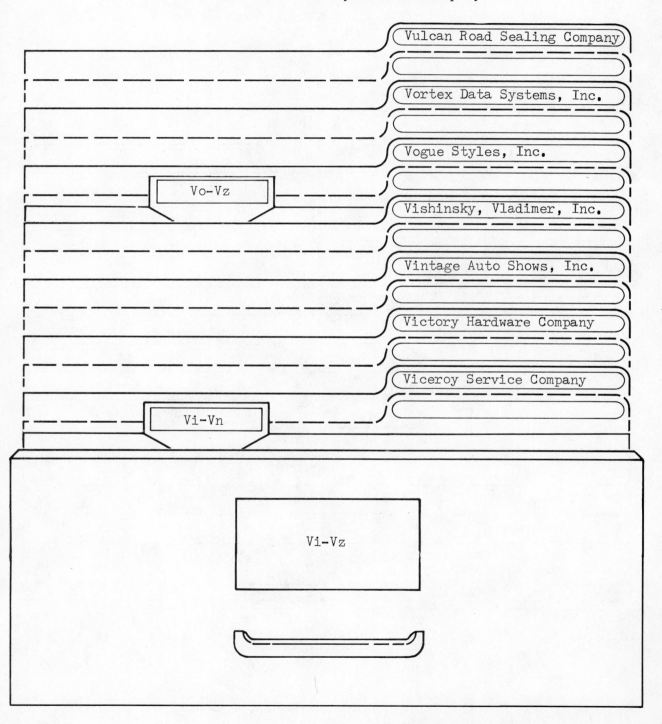

Part 2 • Filing Business Names with Descriptive Words or Personal Names

Notice that *one* of the folders below is *not* in correct alphabetic order. The name on the incorrectly filed folder has been crossed out. Then it has been placed in correct order.

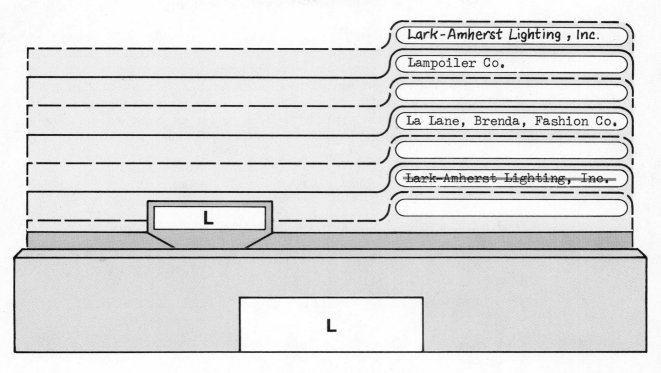

Practice 2: *One* of the folders is *not* in correct alphabetic order. Cross out the name on the incorrectly filed folder. Then place it in correct order.

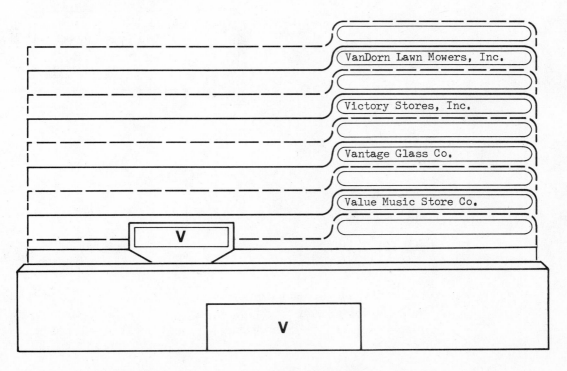

Usually you will use *individual* folders for filing names of persons or businesses. Each person and company has a separate file folder to hold all papers to, from, or about that person or company.

When there are only a few papers for a person or business, a *miscellaneous* folder may be used. Miscellaneous folders hold papers about more than one person or company whose names begin with the same letter. When papers for one person or company reach a certain number (usually three or five), an *individual* folder is then prepared for that person or company. Papers for that person or company are removed from the miscellaneous folder and placed in the new individual folder.

A miscellaneous *A* folder might contain papers like this:

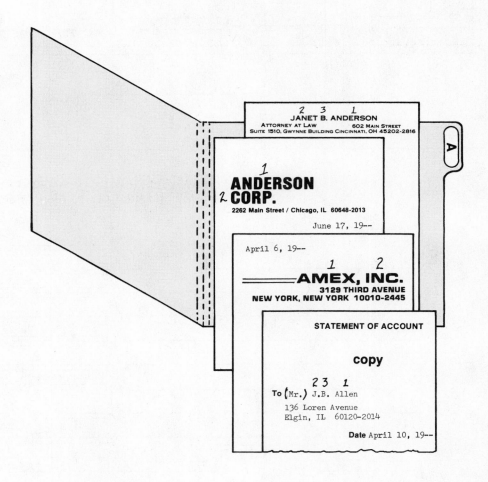

In a file drawer, a file guide starts an alphabetic section, and a miscellaneous folder ends the alphabetic section. The miscellaneous folder is placed *behind* all the individual folders in an alphabetic section of a file drawer.

When you file in a drawer that has individual folders, put papers for people and for companies into folders marked with their names.

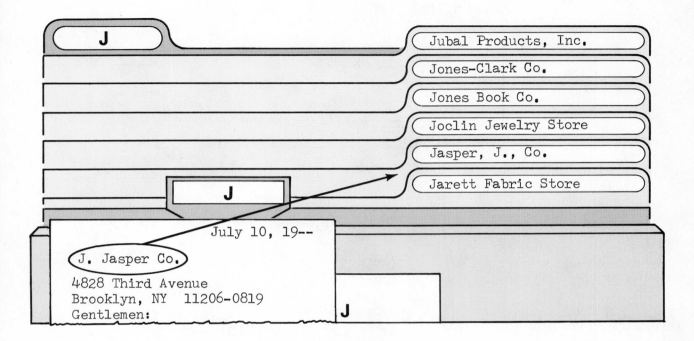

When you file papers for people and for companies that do *not* have individual folders, put the papers in miscellaneous folders.

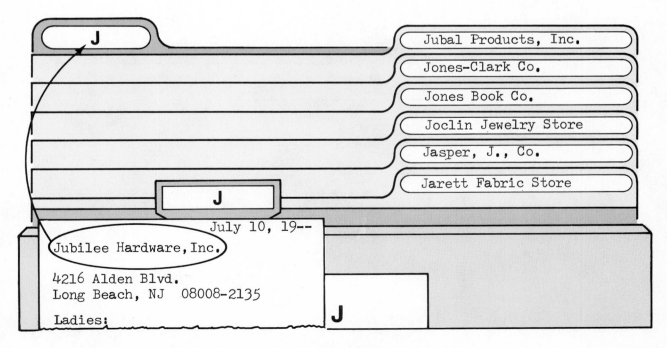

Notice the names on the letters below. At the right is a file drawer that has *individual* and *miscellaneous* folders. Each folder in the drawer has been numbered. As you see, the names on the letters have been coded. The number of the folder in which each of the letters should be placed has been written beside the letters.

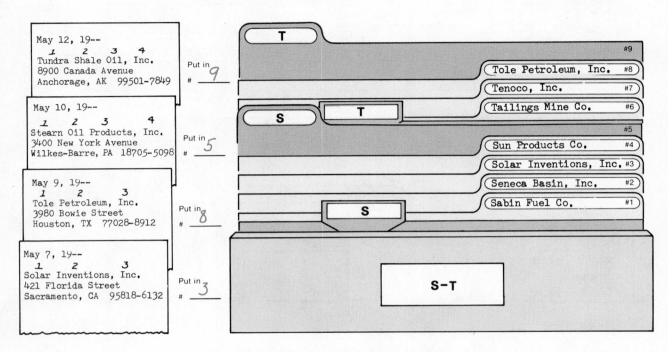

May 12, 19--
1 2 3 4
Tundra Shale Oil, Inc.
8900 Canada Avenue
Anchorage, AK 99501-7849

Put in # _9_

May 10, 19--
1 2 3 4
Stearn Oil Products, Inc.
3400 New York Avenue
Wilkes-Barre, PA 18705-5098

Put in # _5_

May 9, 19--
1 2 3
Tole Petroleum, Inc.
3980 Bowie Street
Houston, TX 77028-8912

Put in # _8_

May 7, 19--
1 2 3
Solar Inventions, Inc.
421 Florida Street
Sacramento, CA 95818-6132

Put in # _3_

Practice 3: Each folder in the file drawer at the right has been numbered. Code the names on the letters at the left. Then write the number of the folder in which each letter should be placed beside the letters.

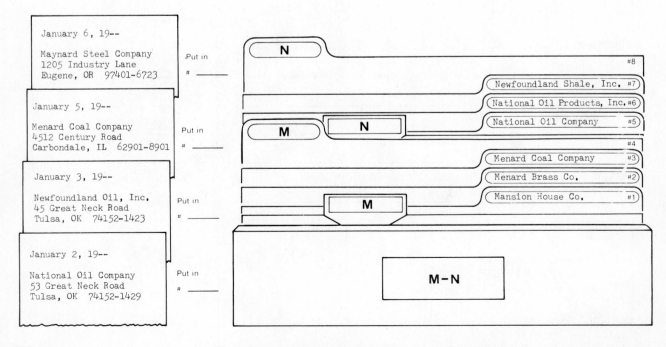

January 6, 19--

Maynard Steel Company
1205 Industry Lane
Eugene, OR 97401-6723

Put in # _____

January 5, 19--

Menard Coal Company
4512 Century Road
Carbondale, IL 62901-8901

Put in # _____

January 3, 19--

Newfoundland Oil, Inc.
45 Great Neck Road
Tulsa, OK 74152-1423

Put in # _____

January 2, 19--

National Oil Company
53 Great Neck Road
Tulsa, OK 74152-1429

Put in # _____

A purchasing department fills out and files purchase orders. Notice that the names on the orders below have been coded. The number of the folder in which each order should be placed has been written beside the order.

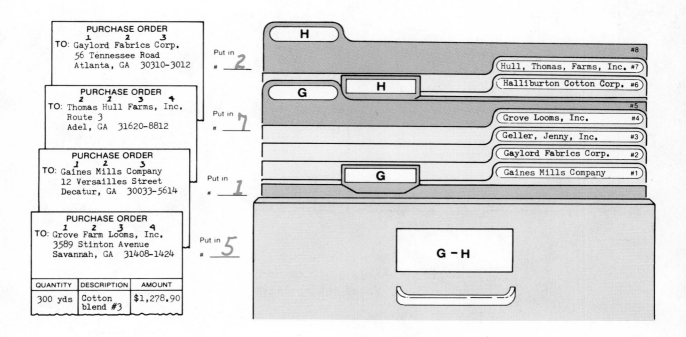

Practice 4: Code the names on the orders below. Then write the number of the folder in which each order should be placed.

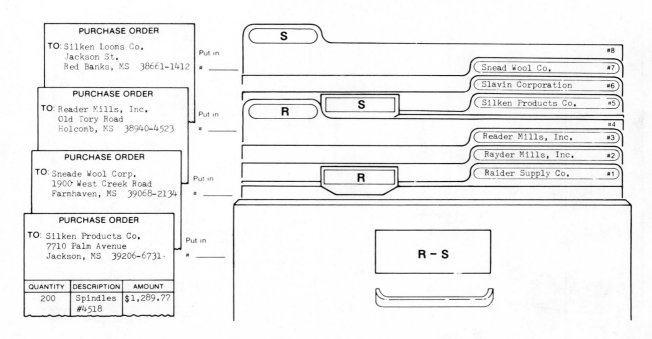

When you file papers in a miscellaneous folder, you should code them and then file them in alphabetic order in the folder. For example, if you had two letters:

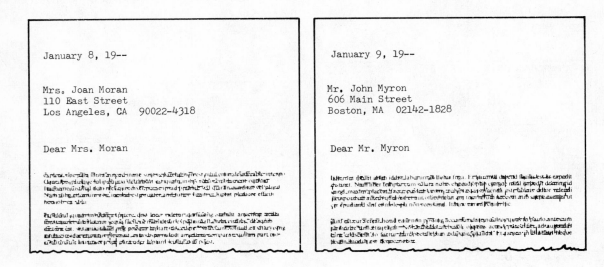

You would file both letters in a miscellaneous *M* folder. The letter to Joan Moran should come *first* in the folder, and the letter to John Myron should be placed *behind* Moran's letter.

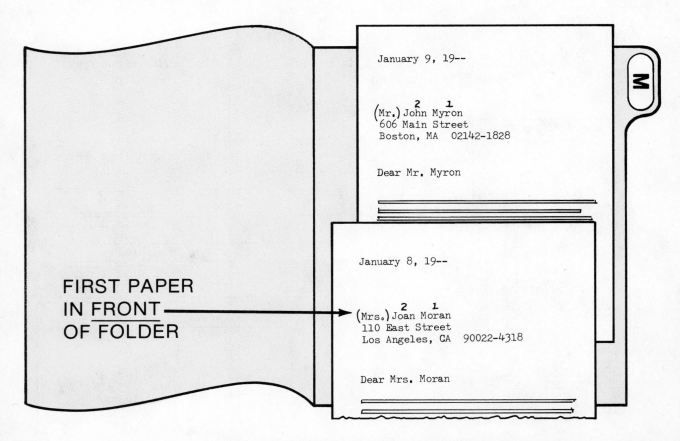

Part 2 • Filing Business Names with Descriptive Words or Personal Names

When you file in a *miscellaneous* folder, arrange the papers alphabetically with the *first* paper at the *front* of the folder. Notice that the names on the orders below have been coded. The order in which the purchase orders should be placed in the miscellaneous folder has been shown by writing the number beside each order.

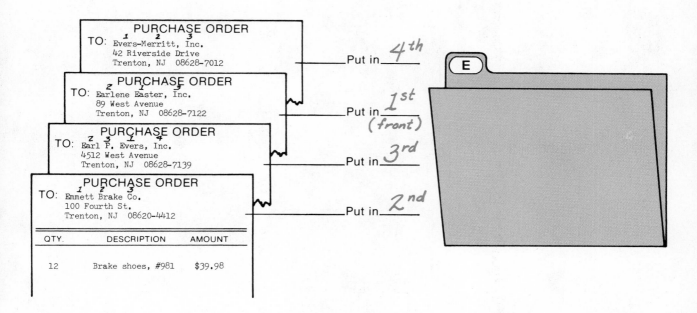

Practice 5: Code the names on the purchase orders below. Then show the order in which the purchase orders should be placed in the miscellaneous folder by writing the number on the line beside each order.

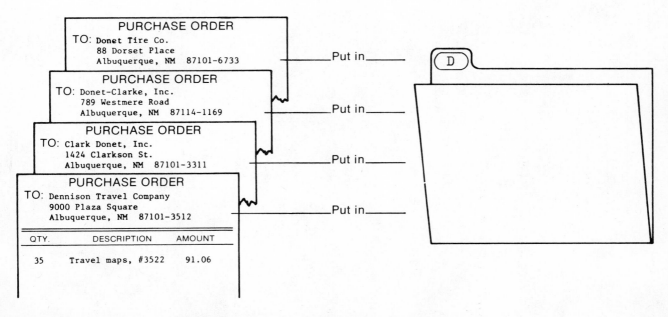

When you file letters in an *individual* folder, file them by date, with the letter having the most recent date in the front of the folder. Filing the letters by date is filing them in *chronologic* order. This is done so that when you open the folder, you can quickly find the most recently filed letter.

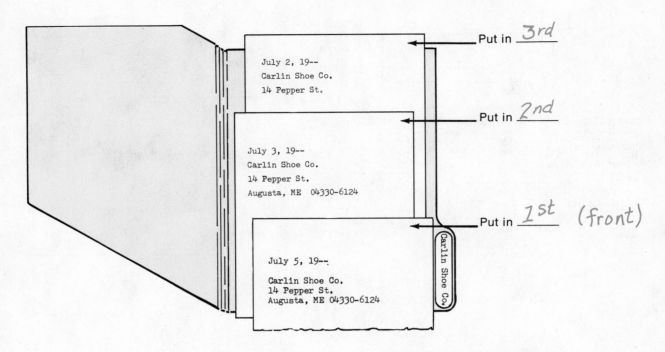

Practice 6: Show the order in which the letters below should be placed in the individual folder by writing the number beside each letter.

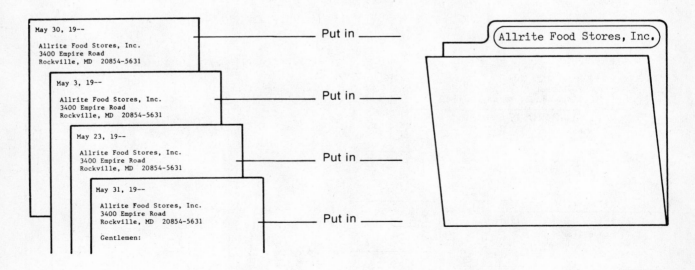

FILING BUSINESS NAMES WITH CONNECTORS OR POSSESSIVES

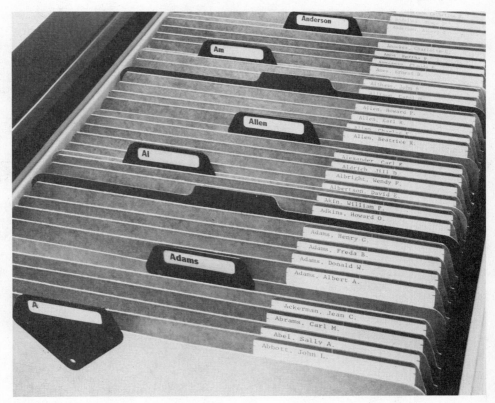

The Shaw-Walker Co.

When you file papers in a business office, you will have to file the names of businesses which are different from those business names you have learned about so far. For example, you might file business names like these:

Sorento and Lewis, Inc.   Kovak's Auto Parts Company
The Studio of Dance, Inc.   Klein and Daughters, Inc.

When you file you will usually find that you use some file folders more than others. To make it easier for you to find folders that you use often, *special guides* are used. The names of the people and businesses that you use most often are written on special guide tabs so that you can quickly spot these folders in the drawer.

Look at the drawer below. Notice that a special guide for the name *Lange* was placed in the third position. This guide will make it easy for you to find the folders with names whose first indexing unit is *Lange*.

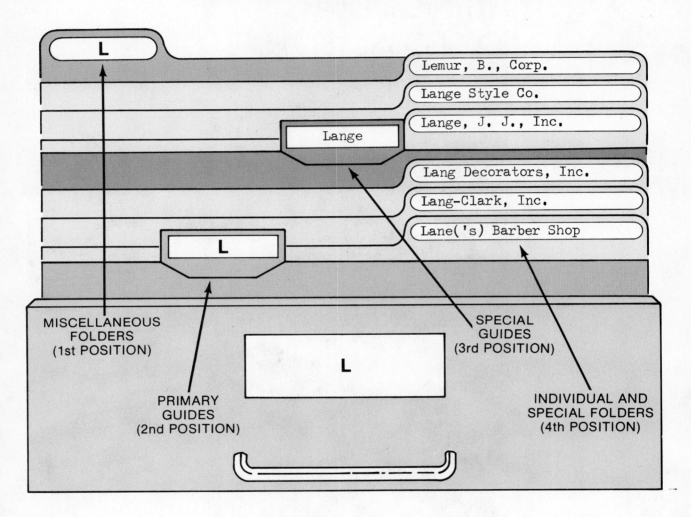

In Part 3 you will learn how to:

1. File the names of businesses such as The Studio of Dance, Inc.
2. Use special guides.
3. File computer and other types of cards.

SECTION 1   BUSINESS NAMES THAT INCLUDE THE

Some business names use the word *the* in their name. *The* may come at the *beginning* or in the *middle* of the name. Here are some examples:

The Helen Baker Co.   Helen the Baker Co.
The Phillip Butcher Corp.   Phillip the Butcher Corp.

When you index such names, do not count *the* as a separate indexing unit. If *the* is the first word in the company name, put it in parentheses ( ) *after* the last indexing unit.

	Indexing Order		
Unarranged Names	Unit 1	Unit 2	Unit 3
The Helen Baker Co.	Baker	Helen	Company (The)
The Phillip Butcher Corp.	Butcher	Phillip	Corporation (The)

If *the* comes in the *middle* of the name, put it in parentheses *next to* the word it follows:

	Indexing Order		
Unarranged Names	Unit 1	Unit 2	Unit 3
Helen the Baker Co.	Helen (the)	Baker	Company
Phillip the Butcher Corp.	Phillip (the)	Butcher	Corporation

You will notice in the names above — *Helen the Baker Co.* and *Phillip the Butcher Corp.* — that you indexed according to the *first* names. That is because there is *no* last name.

The unarranged names below have been indexed.

	Indexing Order		
Unarranged Names	Unit 1	Unit 2	Unit 3
The Cecile Tailor Co.	Tailor	Cecile	Company (The)
Manuel the Tailor	Manuel (the)	Tailor	
The Plaza Carpenter Co.	Plaza	Carpenter	Company (The)
Shirley the Chef, Inc.	Shirley (the)	Chef	Incorporated

Practice 1: Index the unarranged names below.

	Indexing Order		
Unarranged Names	Unit 1	Unit 2	Unit 3
The Fernando Shoemaker Co.	_____	_____	_____
Isabel the Hatmaker	_____	_____	_____
Sharon the Plumber	_____	_____	_____
The Frank Barber Co.	_____	_____	_____

You are now ready to put names with *the* in alphabetic order. The unarranged names below were indexed and then put in alphabetic order.

Unarranged Names	Indexing Order Unit 1	Unit 2	Unit 3
The Josephine Brooks Corp.	Brooks	Josephine	Corporation (The)
Phil the Carpenter	Phil (the)	Carpenter	
The Pamela Carpenter Co.	Carpenter	Pamela	Company (The)

Alphabetic Order

Brooks, Josephine, Corp. (The)
Carpenter, Pamela, Co. (The)
Phil (the) Carpenter

Practice 2: Index the unarranged names below. Then put them in alphabetic order.

Unarranged Names	Indexing Order Unit 1	Unit 2	Unit 3
The Henrietta Daily Co.	_____	_____	_____
Joe the Photographer	_____	_____	_____
The Awilda Diaz Corp.	_____	_____	_____

Alphabetic Order

_____

_____

_____

The *two* unarranged names below were indexed and then placed in alphabetic order in the list of names.

Unarranged Names	Indexing Order Unit 1	Unit 2	Unit 3
The Julia Factor Corp.	Factor	Julia	Corporation (The)
House Improvements, Inc.	House	Improvements	Incorporated

Alphabetic Order

Factor, Arthur, Co. (The)
Factor, Julia, Cap. (The)
Gateway, Joseph, Corp.

House, Harold, Corp. (The)
House Improvements, Inc.

Practice 3: Index the two unarranged names below. Then place them in alphabetic order.

	Indexing Order		
Unarranged Names	**Unit 1**	**Unit 2**	**Unit 3**
The Paul Hawkins Corp.	_____	_____	_____
Margaret the Goldsmith	_____	_____	_____

Alphabetic Order

Haney Home Builders, Inc.

Houseman, Donald, Co. (The)

Jewett, Eloise, Corp. (The)

The unarranged names below have been coded and then placed in alphabetic order.

Unarranged Names

(The) June Goldsmith Co.
   2   1   3

Jonathan (the) Goldsmith, Inc.
1   2   3

Hilda Jacinto, Inc.
 2   1   3

Julio (the) Jeweler, Inc.
1   2   3

Alphabetic Order

Goldsmith, June, Co. (The)
Jacinto, Hilda, Inc.
Jonathan (the) Goldsmith, Inc.
Julio (the) Jeweler, Inc.

Practice 4: Code the unarranged names below. Then place them in alphabetic order.

Unarranged Names	**Alphabetic Order**
The Hyacinth Mason Co.	_____
Morales the Mason, Inc.	_____
Master Messenger Service	_____
The Ronald Masters Co.	_____
The Nickel Coating Corp.	_____

Never Use **The** As An Indexing Unit!

The names below have been coded. If the coding is *correct*, a check mark has been placed in the *Right* column. If the coding is *not* correct, a check mark has been placed in the *Wrong* column.

	Answers	
Coded Names	**Right**	**Wrong**
2 3 1 4		
Amalia J. Lugo Corp.	✓	_____
1 2 3 4		
(The) Helen Mendez Design Showroom	_____	✓
1 2 3 4		
Hazel (the) Furrier, Inc.	_____	✓

Practice 5: The names below have been coded. If the coding is *correct*, place a check mark in the *Right* column. If the coding is *not* correct, place a check mark in the *Wrong* column.

	Answers	
Coded Names	**Right**	**Wrong**
1 2 3 4		
(The) Ace Trucking Service	1. _____	_____
1 2 3 4		
Joel (the) Porter Corporation	2. _____	_____
1 2 3		
(The) Harmony Record Company	3. _____	_____

Integrated Practice G: Code the unarranged names below and then put them in alphabetic order.

Unarranged Names	**Alphabetic Order**
The Boulevard Steel Corp.	_____
Jones the Florist	_____
The Manpower Co.	_____
Manpower Services, Inc.	_____
Jai-Alai Piano Lounge	_____
The Pizza Palace	_____
The Rodrigo Barbera Co.	_____

WHAT HAVE YOU LEARNED IN SECTION 1?

(1) The word <u>the</u> is used as part of many business names.
(2) Do not count the word <u>the</u> as an indexing unit.
(3) Ignore the word <u>the</u> when placing names in alphabetic order.
(4) If the word <u>the</u> comes at the beginning of a company name, write it in parentheses after the last indexing unit.
(5) If the word <u>the</u> comes in the middle of a company name, write it in parentheses after the word it follows.

SECTION 2

BUSINESS NAMES WITH MINOR WORDS AND OTHER ENDINGS

Sometimes a business name may include certain minor words that are not names and do not describe the kind of business. The most common minor word used in business names is *and* or *&*. Other minor words are *of, by, to,* and *for*.

These minor words do not add meaning to a business name and are not used as indexing units. To show that these minor words are not used as indexing units, they are placed in parentheses. Here are some examples:

	Indexing Order		
Unarranged Names	**Unit 1**	**Unit 2**	**Unit 3**
Smedley and Robinson, Inc.	Smedley (and)	Robinson	Incorporated
Heather & Jonas, Architects	Heather (&)	Jonas	Architects
Photographs by Sylvia	Photographs (by)	Sylvia	
Denton of Engelwood	Denton (of)	Engelwood	

When such minor words as *at, in*, etc., are *meaningful first units* of a business name, they are shown as the first indexing unit. Here are some examples:

	Indexing Order			
Unarranged Names	**Unit 1**	**Unit 2**	**Unit 3**	**Unit 4**
In the Mood Record Store	In (the)	Mood	Record	Store
At the Seashore Restaurant	At (the)	Seashore	Restaurant	
On the Town Clothing Store	On (the)	Town	Clothing	Store

You may also find business firms that add the word *Son* or *Sons;* *Daughter* or *Daughters; Brother* or *Brothers*; or *Sister* or *Sisters* to the company name. These words are indexed in the order written. Here are some examples of such names:

Unarranged Names	Indexing Order			
	Unit 1	**Unit 2**	**Unit 3**	**Unit 4**
John Simpson & Daughter	Simpson	John (&)	Daughter	
Viola Taylor & Sons, Inc.	Taylor	Viola (&)	Sons	Incorporated
Roberto R. Sanchez & Son	Sanchez	Roberto	R. (&)	Son
Roberts & Brothers Jewelry	Roberts (&)	Brothers	Jewelry	

The unarranged names below have been indexed and placed in alphabetic order.

Unarranged Names

1. Hattie Brownfeld & Sons
2. L. C. Bruning & Daughters
3. Gibson & Santiago, Ltd.

Indexing Order				
Unit 1	**Unit 2**	**Unit 3**	**Unit 4**	**Alphabetic Order**
1. Brownfeld	Hattie (&)	Sons		Brownfeld, Hattie (&) Sons
2. Bruning	L.	C. (&)	Daughters	Bruning, L. C., (&) Daughters
3. Gibson (&)	Santiago	Limited		Gibson (&) Santiago, Ltd.

Practice 1: Index the unarranged names below. Then put them in alphabetic order.

Unarranged Names

1. Kingsley, Kramer & Horner
2. L. S. Keily and Brothers
3. Diana Keilly & Son, Inc.

Indexing Order				
Unit 1	**Unit 2**	**Unit 3**	**Unit 4**	**Alphabetic Order**
1. _____	_____	_____	_____	_____
2. _____	_____	_____	_____	_____
3. _____	_____	_____	_____	_____

The unarranged names below have been indexed and then placed in alphabetic order in the list of names at the right.

Unarranged Names

1. Steiner & Sons, Inc.
2. Bella Swartz & Associates

	Indexing Order		
Unit 1	**Unit 2**	**Unit 3**	**Alphabetic Order**
1. Steiner (&)	Sons	Incorporated	
2. Swartz	Bella (&)	Associates	

Alphabetic Order

Steinbrand, Gary, (&) Son

Steiner (&) Sons, Inc.

Styles (by) Phyllis, Inc.

Swartz, Bella, (&) Associates

Swartz, Herman (&) Lin, Inc.

_____

Swenson (&) Sons, Inc.

Practice 2: Index the unarranged names below and then place them in alphabetic order in the list at the right.

Unarranged Names

1. Anton & Kleiner, Inc.
2. R. L. Koenig, Ltd.

	Indexing Order			
Unit 1	**Unit 2**	**Unit 3**	**Unit 4**	**Alphabetic Order**
1. _____	_____	_____	_____	
2. _____	_____	_____	_____	

Alphabetic Order

Anton (&) Walton, Inc.

Klein, Alice, Corp.

Kleinman, Annette, (&) Daughters, Inc.

Kuhn, Anita, (&) Sons, Inc.

Kuhn, Joseph, Company

_____

The unarranged names below have been coded. If the coding is *correct*, a check mark has been placed in the *Right* column. If the coding is *not* correct, a check mark has been placed in the *Wrong* column. Incorrectly coded names have been coded correctly below. Then all the names have been placed in correct alphabetic order.

	Answers	
Unarranged Names	**Right**	**Wrong**

2   1   3 4 5

Amanda Suarez (&) Son, Inc.   _____ ✓ _____

2 1   3

L. Nagaka (&) Brothers   ✓ _____ _____

         1   2 3

(The) Chelsea Co., Inc.   ✓ _____ _____

Corrected Coding

Amanda Suarez (&) Son, Inc. (handwritten, coded: 2 1 3 4)

Alphabetic Order

Chelsea Co., Inc. (The)
Nagaka, L., (&) Brothers
Suarez, Amanda, (&) Son, Inc.

Practice 3: The unarranged names below have been coded. If the coding is *correct*, place a check mark in the *Right* column. If the coding is *not* correct, place a check mark in the *Wrong* column. Then code correctly any incorrectly coded names and place all the names in correct alphabetic order below.

	Answers	
Unarranged Names	**Right**	**Wrong**

1   2   3   4

Patricia Potter (&) Son, Inc.   1. _____ _____

1   2   3

Peter (the) Stylist, Inc.   2. _____ _____

2 1   3   4

J. Prinz (&) Son, Ltd.   3. _____ _____

1   2   3

Haynes, Liu (&) Harwood   4. _____ _____

Corrected Coding

_____

_____

_____

_____

Alphabetic Order

_____

_____

_____

_____

Name: _____

One of the names below was placed in *incorrect* alphabetic order because it was coded incorrectly. That name was crossed out and coded correctly. Then it was put in *correct* alphabetic order.

Unarranged Names

1   2   3
Harwood (&) Jamison, Ltd.
1   2   3   4
Howard H. Hardesty, Inc.
1   2   3
Jill (the) Stylist, Inc.

Corrected Coding

2   3   1   4
Howard H. Hardesty, Inc.

Alphabetic Order

Hardesty, Howard H., Inc.

Harwood (&) Jamison, Ltd.

~~Howard H. Hardesty, Inc.~~

Jill (the) Stylist, Inc.

Practice 4: Find the name that is in *incorrect* alphabetic order at the right. Cross out that name, code it correctly, and then place it in *correct* alphabetic order.

Unarranged Names

1 2   3   4   5
W. W. Simmons (&) Sons Manufacturing
2 3   1   4
Will W. Simonson Corporation
2   1   3 4
Mary Seeley (&) Co., Inc.

Corrected Coding

_____

Alphabetic Order

Seeley, Mary, (&) Co., Inc.

Simonson, Will W., Corporation

W. W. Simmons (&) Sons Manufacturing

Code the unarranged names below and then put them in alphabetic order.

Unarranged Names	**Alphabetic Order**
Sharon Reynolds & Son, Inc.	_____
On the Road Trucking Co.	_____
Jack Reynolds-Baker & Company	_____
The House of Pancakes	_____
F. L. Rhodes and Daughters	_____
Jill Rhodes & Brothers, Inc.	_____
The Roade Sisters Carpet Cleaners	_____
F. Lila Rodman, Ltd.	_____
James Lin & Brothers Corp.	_____
The Seaside Drug Co.	_____
From the Farm Produce Co.	_____
Hannah Baker Office Supplies	_____

WHAT HAVE YOU LEARNED IN SECTION 2?

(1) Business names may include minor words such as <u>and</u>, <u>of</u>, <u>by</u>, <u>to</u>, and <u>for</u>. Such words are not counted as separate indexing units. They are written in parentheses.
(2) When a minor word such as <u>at</u>, <u>on</u>, <u>in</u>, etc., is a meaningful first unit of a business name, it is used as the first indexing unit.
(3) Business names which include <u>Daughter(s)</u>, <u>Son(s)</u>, <u>Brother(s)</u>, or <u>Sister(s)</u> are indexed in the order in which they are written.

SECTION 3   BUSINESS NAMES WITH '<u>S</u> OR <u>S</u>'

You have learned in your English classes that you show that something belongs to someone (possession) by using the apostrophe ('). However, some people do not clearly understand whether to put the apostrophe (') *before* or *after* the S. The apostrophe usually goes *before* the S, as in the following examples:

Roberta's Book
Jose's Shirt
Stanton's Company

If the word to which you want to add the apostrophe (') already ends in S, simply add the apostrophe (') *after* the S as in the following examples:

Harris' Tools
Iris' Pencil
Lois' Shoes

When you index and alphabetize business names that contain an apostrophe S ('S) to show possession, put the 'S in parentheses ('S). This is done because the S is not part of the original name. Here are some examples of how to index such names:

	Indexing Order		
Unarranged Names	**Unit 1**	**Unit 2**	**Unit 3**
Byron's Specialty Stores	Byron('s)	Specialty	Stores
Milt Sawyer's & Sons	Sawyer('s)	Milt (&)	Sons

When a business name ends in S', you *do* use the S in indexing and alphabetizing because it is part of the original name. Here is the way you would index the following names ending in S':

	Indexing Order			
Unarranged Names	**Unit 1**	**Unit 2**	**Unit 3**	**Unit 4**
Lucas' Department Stores	Lucas'	Department	Stores	
James' Home Furnishings Corp.	James'	Home	Furnishings	Corporation

You are now ready to index and alphabetize names containing a possessive — either 'S or S'. Even though the name is written in full, ignore the 'S (which is written in parentheses) when you are putting names in alphabetic order.

The unarranged names below have been indexed and then put in alphabetic order.

Unarranged Names

1. Arthur Henry's Toys, Inc.
2. Frieda Douglas' Real Estate
3. Barnes & Douglas, Inc.
4. Rita C. Thomas' Homes

Indexing Order

Unit 1	Unit 2	Unit 3	Unit 4	Alphabetic Order
1. Henry('s)	Arthur	Toys	Incorporated	Barnes (&) Douglas, Inc.
2. Douglas'	Frieda	Real	Estate	Douglas', Frieda, Real Estate
3. Barnes (&)	Douglas	Incorporated		Henry('s), Arthur, Toys, Inc.
4. Thomas'	Rita	C.	Homes	Thomas', Rita C., Homes

Practice 1: Index the unarranged names below and then put them in alphabetic order.

Unarranged Names

1. Beatrice Henry's Flowers
2. Ina Morris' Insurance Agency
3. The Santos Brothers Trucking Co.
4. Peter Gould & Sons Furniture

Indexing Order

Unit 1	Unit 2	Unit 3	Unit 4	Alphabetic Order
1. _____	_____	_____	_____	_____
2. _____	_____	_____	_____	_____
3. _____	_____	_____	_____	_____
4. _____	_____	_____	_____	_____

The unarranged name below has been coded. Then the name has been placed in alphabetic order in the list of names at the right.

Unarranged Name	Alphabetic Order
1 2 3	
Howards' Music Store	_____
	Harwood, Arthur, (&) Sons
	_____
	Howard('s) Dump Trucks
	_____
	Howard, E. J., (&) Sisters
	Howards' Music Store

Practice 2: Code the unarranged name below. Then put it in alphabetic order in the list of names at the right.

Unarranged Name   **Alphabetic Order**

Reynold's Clothing, Inc.

_____

Reynolds' Building Materials, Ltd.

_____

Reynolds, Pat, (&) Daughter, Designers

_____

Reynolds (&) Patrick Corporation

_____

The unarranged names below have been coded. If the coding is *correct*, a check mark has been placed in the *Right* column. If the coding is *not* correct, a check mark has been placed in the *Wrong* column.

	Answers	
Unarranged Names	**Right**	**Wrong**
1 2 3		
Rojas (&) Jiminez, Ltd.	✓	
1 2 3 4		
Hector Rojas' Lamps, Inc.		✓
1 2 3		
Robert('s) Laundry Corp.	✓	
1 2 3		
(The) Roberts Book Company	✓	

Practice 3: The unarranged names below have been coded. If the coding is *correct*, place a check mark in the *Right* column. If the coding is *not* correct, place a check mark in the *Wrong* column.

	Answers	
Unarranged Names	**Right**	**Wrong**
1 2 3		
Laurel('s) Paintings (&) Prints	1. _____	_____
2 1 3 4		
(The) J. Hilton (&) Son Co.	2. _____	_____
2 1 3		
(The) Edie Carrol Corporation	3. _____	_____
1 2 3 4		
Eddy('s) Expert Auto Repair	4. _____	_____
1 2 3		
Eddy('s) Delivery Service	5. _____	_____

Integrated Practice I: Code the unarranged names below and then put them in alphabetic order.

Unarranged Names	Alphabetic Order
The Hayes-Greb Co.	_____
Dance with Olga	_____
Gordon's Shirt Shop	_____
Jane Hayes & Daughters, Inc.	_____
In & Out Food Mart	_____
Harris' Books, Inc.	_____
Bob Harris & Son Bedding Co.	_____
The Greta Hayes Outlet Store	_____
Hayes' Purchasing Service	_____
Annie Gordon's Shops, Ltd.	_____
Allen the Computer Bug	_____

WHAT HAVE YOU LEARNED IN SECTION 3?

(1) A business name may include a possessive ('S or S').
(2) If a business name is written with an apostrophe S ('S), do <u>not</u> use the S in indexing or alphabetizing. This is because the S is not part of the original name.
(3) If a business name is written with an S', you <u>do</u> use the S in indexing and alphabetizing. This is because the S is part of the original name.

SECTION 4   SIMULATED OFFICE PROBLEMS

Notice that the unarranged names below have been coded. Then they have been placed in alphabetic order on the file folder labels.

Unarranged Names

	1	2	3		2	1	3	4
(The)	Hall	(of)	Fame, Inc.	J.	Howard('s)		Clothing	Store

	1	2	3		1	2	3
Hall	(and)	Sons, Inc.		Huff	(and)	Puff, Inc.	

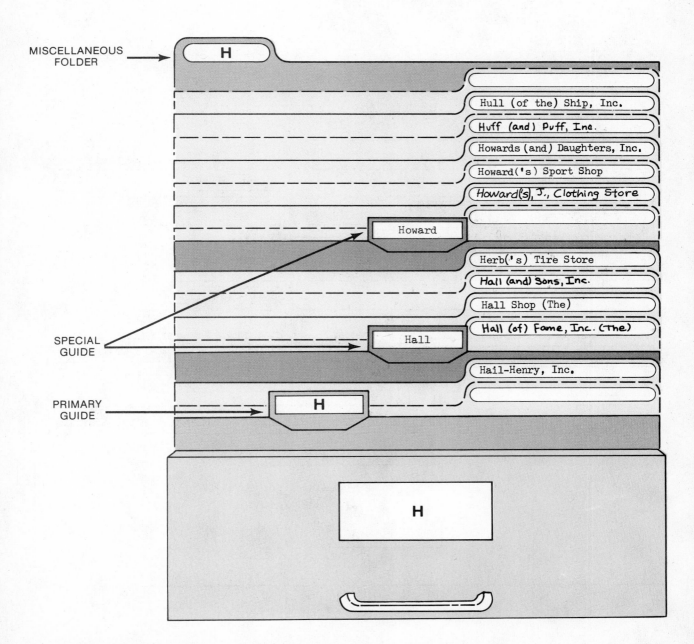

MISCELLANEOUS FOLDER

H

Hull (of the) Ship, Inc.

Huff (and) Puff, Inc.

Howards (and) Daughters, Inc.

Howard('s) Sport Shop

Howard(s), J., Clothing Store

Howard

Herb('s) Tire Store

Hall (and) Sons, Inc.

Hall Shop (The)

Hall (of) Fame, Inc. (The)

Hall

Hail-Henry, Inc.

SPECIAL GUIDE

PRIMARY GUIDE

H

H

Practice 1: Code the unarranged names below. Then write them on the file folder labels below in alphabetic order. Use the primary and special guides to help you.

Unarranged Names

Jerry Cannion Company

Carter-Lee Company

Bailey's Marina

Baileys' Boat Company

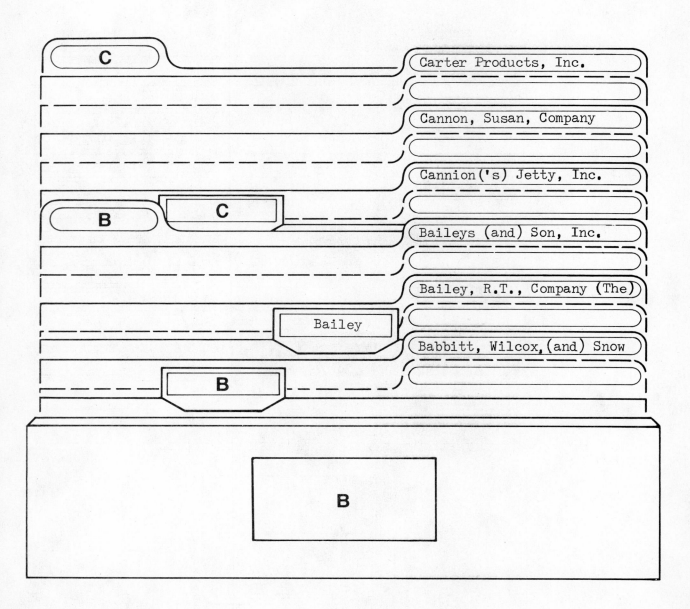

Sometimes when you file letters and papers in a *miscellaneous* folder, there may be two letters about the same business or person. In that case, file the letters about the same business or person by *date*, with the *most recent* date in front, or first.

Notice that the names on the letters below have been coded. Then a number has been written beside each letter to show the order in which it should be placed in the folder.

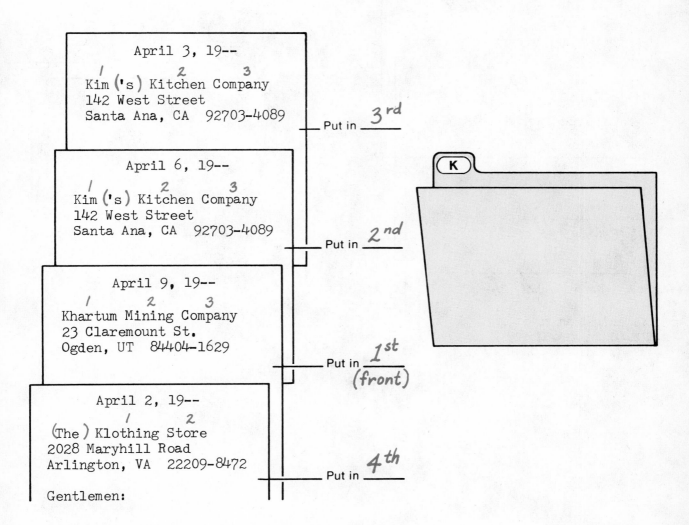

Practice 2: Code the names on the letters below. Then show the order in which the letters would be placed in the miscellaneous folder by writing the number on the line beside each letter.

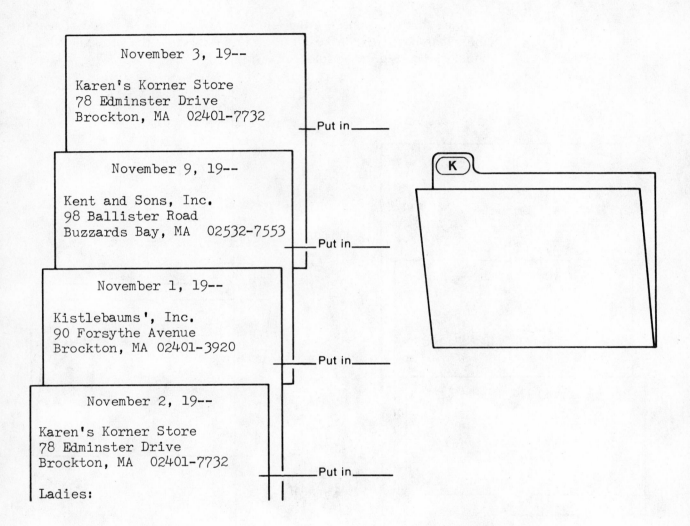

November 3, 19--

Karen's Korner Store
78 Edminster Drive
Brockton, MA 02401-7732

Put in_____

November 9, 19--

Kent and Sons, Inc.
98 Ballister Road
Buzzards Bay, MA 02532-7553

Put in_____

November 1, 19--

Kistlebaums', Inc.
90 Forsythe Avenue
Brockton, MA 02401-3920

Put in_____

November 2, 19--

Karen's Korner Store
78 Edminster Drive
Brockton, MA 02401-7732

Ladies:

Put in_____

K

Notice that the names on the letters below have been coded. Then a number has been written beside each letter to show the order in which it would be placed in the miscellaneous folder.

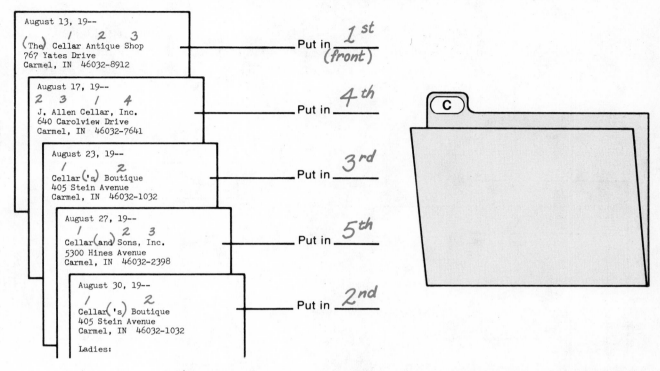

Practice 3: Code the names on the letters below. Then show the order in which the letters would be placed in the miscellaneous folder by writing the number on the line beside each letter.

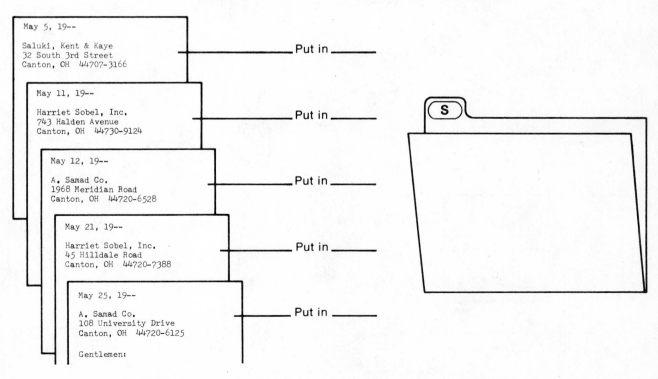

You have learned to file letters in an *individual* folder by date, with the most recent date first, or in front. You do this so that when you open the folder, it is easy to find the most recent letter you filed.

The letters below should be filed in an individual folder because they are all from the same company. Notice that a number has been written beside each letter to show the order in which it should be placed in the folder at the right.

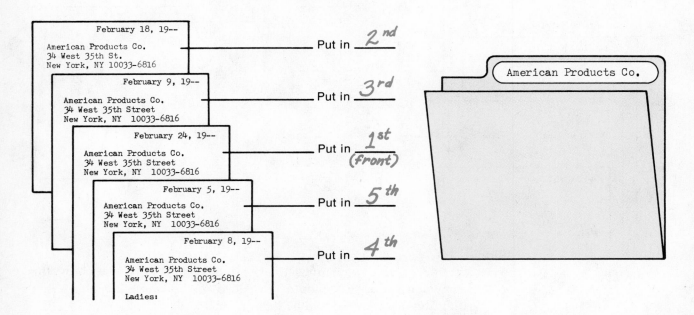

Practice 4: Show the order in which the letters below would be placed in an individual folder by writing the number beside each letter.

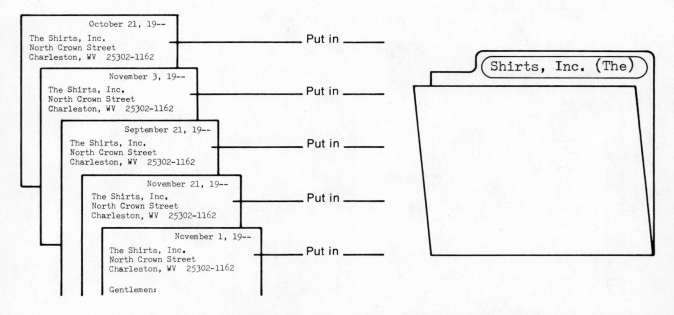

Now you are ready to place papers (Sales Invoices) in a file drawer that contains both *individual* folders and *miscellaneous* folders. Notice that the names on the invoices below have been coded. Then a number has been written beside each invoice to show the folder in which it would be placed.

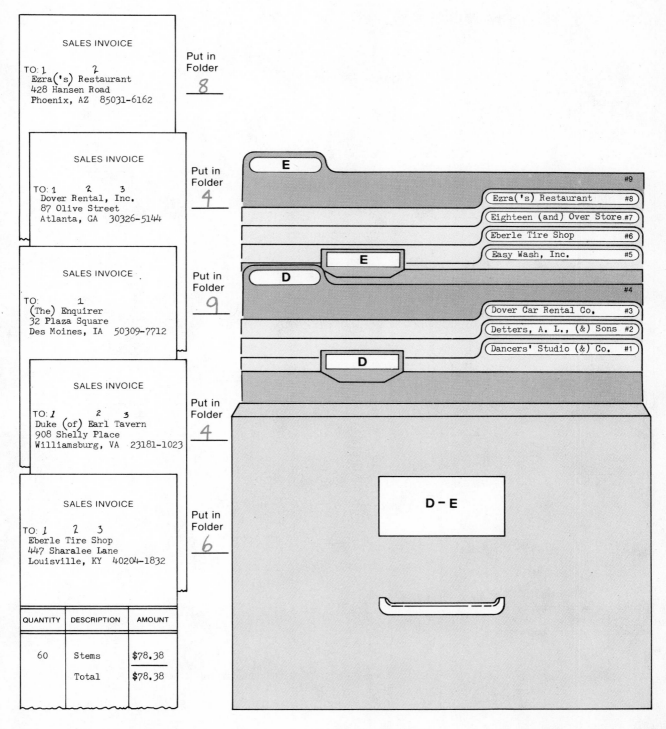

SALES INVOICE

TO: 1   2
Ezra('s) Restaurant
428 Hansen Road
Phoenix, AZ 85031-6162

Put in Folder
8

SALES INVOICE

TO: 1   2   3
Dover Rental, Inc.
87 Olive Street
Atlanta, GA 30326-5144

Put in Folder
4

SALES INVOICE

TO: 1
(The) Enquirer
32 Plaza Square
Des Moines, IA 50309-7712

Put in Folder
9

SALES INVOICE

TO: 1   2   3
Duke (of) Earl Tavern
908 Shelly Place
Williamsburg, VA 23181-1023

Put in Folder
4

SALES INVOICE

TO: 1   2   3
Eberle Tire Shop
447 Sharalee Lane
Louisville, KY 40204-1832

Put in Folder
6

QUANTITY	DESCRIPTION	AMOUNT
60	Stems	$78.38
	Total	$78.38

E

#9

Ezra('s) Restaurant #8

Eighteen (and) Over Store #7

Eberle Tire Shop #6

Easy Wash, Inc. #5

E

D

#4

Dover Car Rental Co. #3

Detters, A. L., (&) Sons #2

Dancers' Studio (&) Co. #1

D

D - E

Practice 5: Code the names on the invoices below. Then show the folder in which the invoices would be placed by writing the number of the folder beside each invoice.

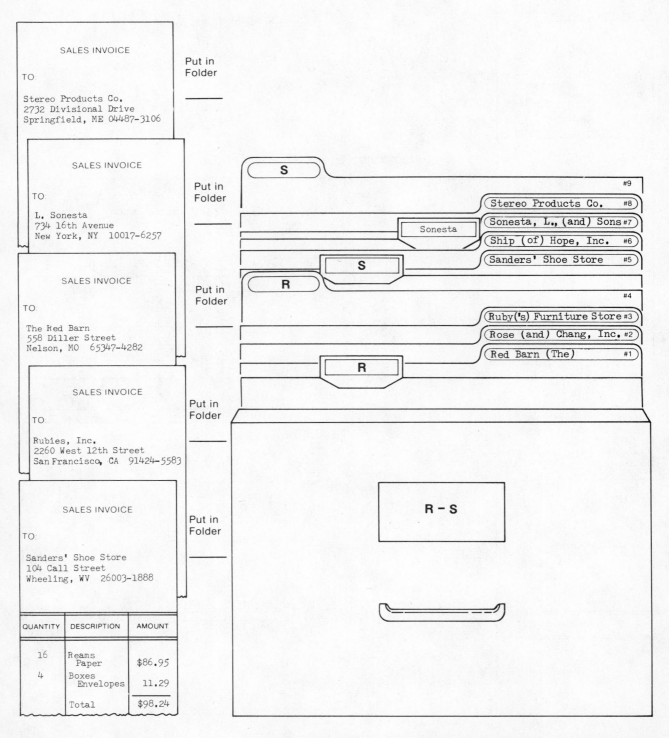

SALES INVOICE

TO:

Stereo Products Co.
2732 Divisional Drive
Springfield, ME 04487-3106

Put in Folder
_____

SALES INVOICE

TO:

L. Sonesta
734 16th Avenue
New York, NY 10017-6257

Put in Folder
_____

SALES INVOICE

TO:

The Red Barn
558 Diller Street
Nelson, MO 65347-4282

Put in Folder
_____

SALES INVOICE

TO:

Rubies, Inc.
2260 West 12th Street
San Francisco, CA 91424-5583

Put in Folder
_____

SALES INVOICE

TO:

Sanders' Shoe Store
104 Call Street
Wheeling, WV 26003-1888

Put in Folder
_____

QUANTITY	DESCRIPTION	AMOUNT
16	Reams Paper	$86.95
4	Boxes Envelopes	11.29
	Total	$98.24

S

#9

Stereo Products Co. #8

Sonesta, L., (and) Sons #7

Sonesta

Ship (of) Hope, Inc. #6

S

Sanders' Shoe Store #5

R

#4

Ruby('s) Furniture Store #3

Rose (and) Chang, Inc. #2

Red Barn (The) #1

R

R – S

To find a telephone number or the name and address of a customer quickly, many office workers use a rotary card file like the one below.

Courtesy of Bostitch Division of Textron Inc.

The rotary card file uses small cards that look like this:

Times (of) Olde, Inc.
23 West Street
Hartford, CT 06114-1365

203 345-7809

The cards snap on to the rings in the rotary card file as shown below.

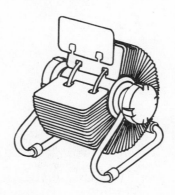

Notice that the names below have been coded. Then they have been written on the rotary file cards in alphabetic order.

Names

Steer(&)Daughters
¹ ²

(The)Steer Salon
¹ ²

J. Clarke Steer, Inc.
² ³ ¹ ⁴

Steer-Clark, Inc.
¹ ² ³

Steer(s) Emporium
¹ ²

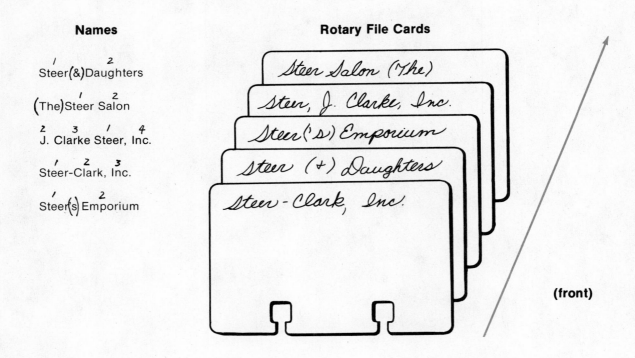

Rotary File Cards

Steer Salon (The)
Steer, J. Clarke, Inc.
Steer('s) Emporium
Steer (+) Daughters
Steer - Clark, Inc.

(front)

Practice 6: Code the names below. Then write the names in correct alphabetic order on the rotary file cards.

Names

Marks of Wood, Inc.

The Marks' Service Co.

Mark's Village Store

Mark R. Wood, Inc.

Julia Marks, Inc.

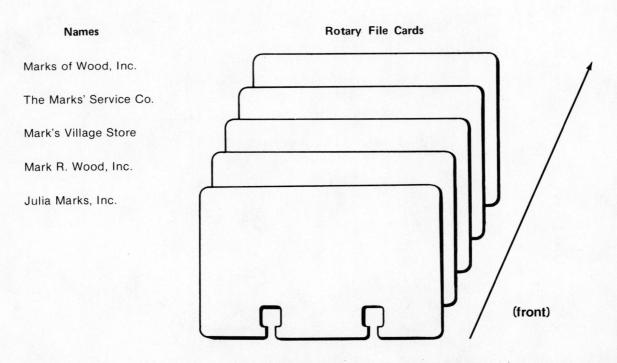

Rotary File Cards

(front)

If you worked in the data processing department of a business, you might file computer cards like this one:

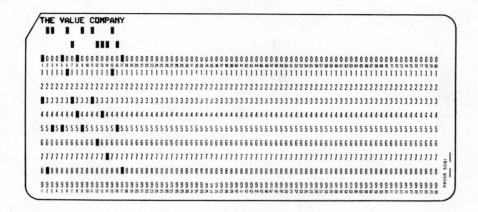

Notice that the names below have been coded. Then they have been placed in alphabetic order in the computer card file by writing the names on the correct blank cards.

2 3   1   4   1   2   3
R. M. VanPlank, Inc.   (The) Very Most Shop

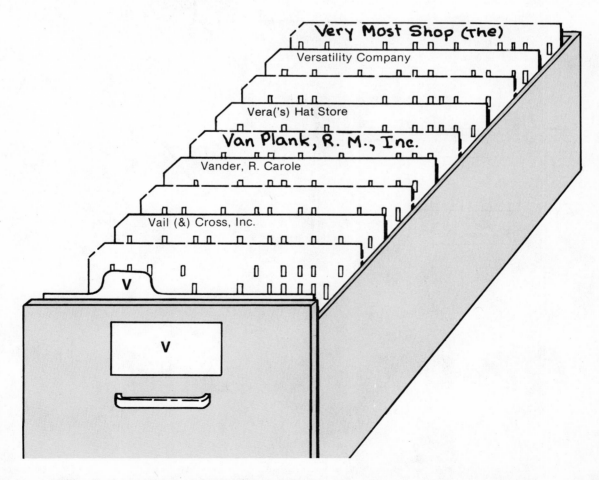

Practice 7: Code the names below. Then place the names in alphabetic order in the card file by writing the names on the correct blank cards.

Harold A. Tim   Maria Teresa, Inc.

The Top Store, Inc.   Tea for Two Tea Co.

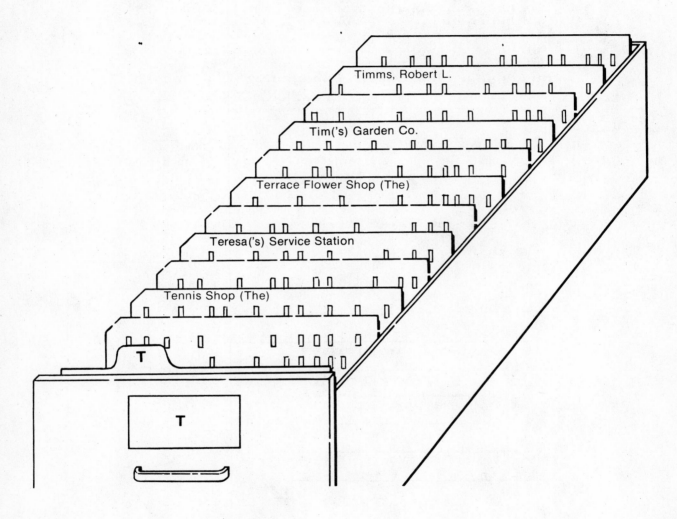

Notice that two computer cards have been filed incorrectly in the file drawer below. The incorrectly filed names have been crossed out. Then they have been placed in correct order.

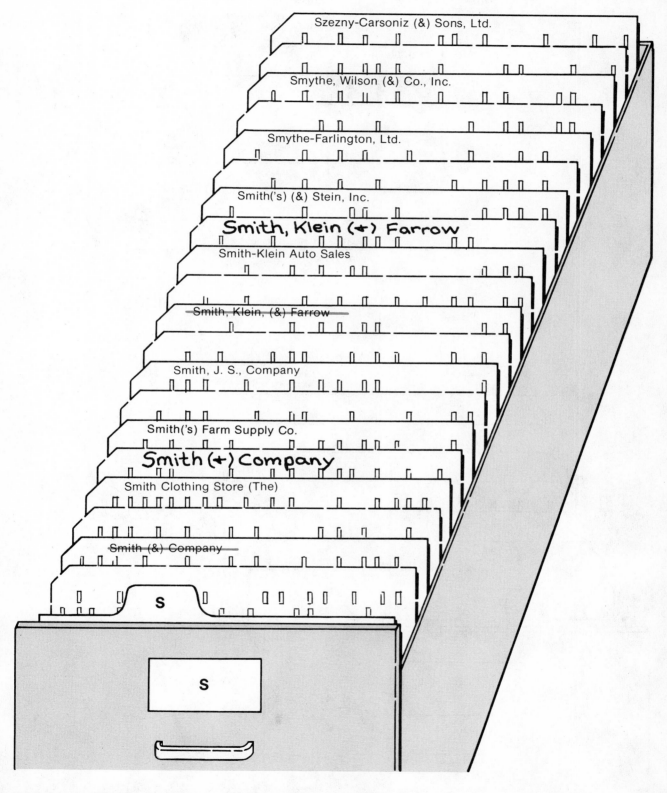

Practice 8: Two computer cards have been filed incorrectly in the file drawer below. Cross out the incorrectly filed names. Then put them in correct alphabetic order.

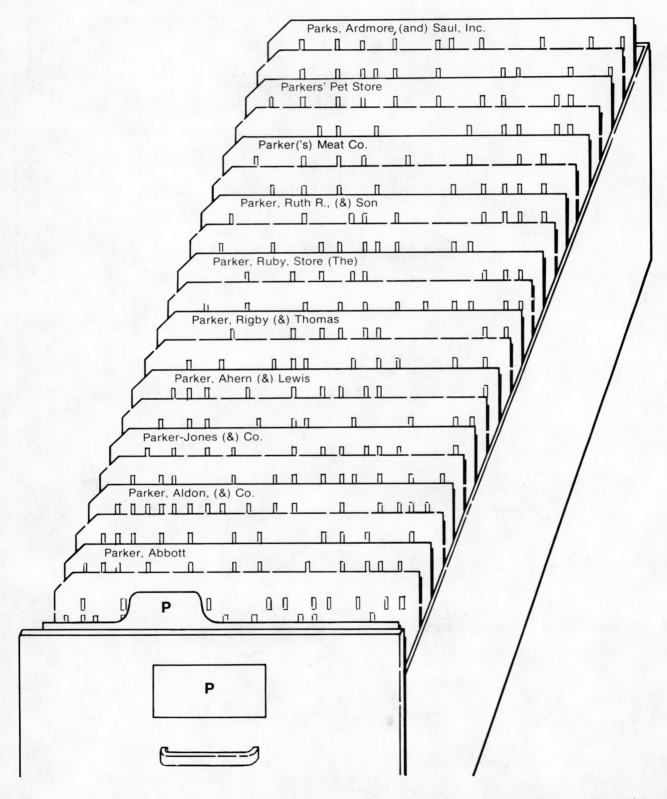

Parks, Ardmore, (and) Saul, Inc.

Parkers' Pet Store

Parker('s) Meat Co.

Parker, Ruth R., (&) Son

Parker, Ruby, Store (The)

Parker, Rigby (&) Thomas

Parker, Ahern (&) Lewis

Parker-Jones (&) Co.

Parker, Aldon, (&) Co.

Parker, Abbott

P

P

PART 4

FILING OTHER BUSINESS NAMES

There are many ways to find office work. One way is to go to your business teacher or guidance counselor for help. You may also find out about jobs from friends and relatives. Another way is to answer the want ads in the newspapers.

One good place to find out about jobs is your State Employment Service. A State Employment Office can usually be found in most large towns and cities.

The State Employment Service can be of special help if you want to find work in a government office.

When you go to the State Employment Service in your town, you will talk with a counselor. The counselor will discuss with you the kind of work you would like as well as the training and skills you have.

The counselor will then arrange an interview for you at a company or government agency. You will find that your ability to file personal and business names will be very important in getting a good office job.

When you are ready to look for a job, ask your teacher for the name and address of the nearest State Employment Office or look in the telephone directory.

BUR OF EMPLYMNT SERVS
Administrative Ofcs 145 S Front
    Genl Information - -------466-4636
    Ohio Claims Information - -466-4348
    Out-Of-State Claims
        Information - ---------466-3548
    Cols Claims Ofc see
              Cols Unemployment Claims
    Contributions-Tax
        Information - ---------466-2319
  Personnel - --------------466-3110
  Asst Attorney Genl - -------466-2707
  Bd Of Review

SECTION 1   ABBREVIATIONS IN BUSINESS NAMES

You have learned that some personal names have only an initial as the first or middle name. When you indexed such names, you counted the initial as a separate indexing unit.

When a business name includes an initial as part of a person's name, you still count the initial as a separate unit in indexing.

In some business names, a few letters are used as an *abbreviation* (shorter form) of a full name. Here are some examples:

Chas.	— Charles	Theo.	— Theodore
Wm.	— William	Jas.	— James
Robt.	— Robert	Thos.	— Thomas
Geo.	— George	Jos.	— Joseph

When you are indexing names that contain such abbreviations, count the abbreviations as separate indexing units. However, in indexing and alphabetizing, write the names out in *full*. When the brief form of a first name (Don, Ed, Liz, Lizzy, Pat, Patty, etc.) is used, the brief form is indexed as it is spelled. Here are some examples:

Indexing Order

Unarranged Names	Unit 1	Unit 2	Unit 3	Unit 4
Chas. Henry & Sons, Inc.	Henry	Charles (&)	Sons	Incorporated
Geo. Williams Corp.	Williams	George	Corporation	
Ted Roberts & Sons, Inc.	Roberts	Ted (&)	Sons	Incorporated
Patty Brennan Accounting	Brennan	Patty	Accounting	

Alphabetic Order

Brennan, Patty, Accounting
Henry, Charles, (&) Sons, Inc.
Roberts, Ted, (&) Sons, Inc.
Williams, George, Corp.

Sometimes business names have single letters that are *not* abbreviations of names. *Each letter* is treated as a separate indexing unit. Hyphens are disregarded. Here are some examples:

Indexing Order

Unarranged Names	Unit 1	Unit 2	Unit 3	Unit 4	Unit 5
ABC Deliveries, Inc.	A	B	C	Deliveries	Incorporated
The O-K Fruit Suppliers	O-	K	Fruit	Suppliers (The)	
The RFD Corp.	R	F	D	Corporation (The)	

In the example below the unarranged names have been indexed and placed in alphabetic order.

Unarranged Names

1. The XYZ Blouse Co.
2. The Jos. Smiley Lock Co.
3. Liz Harris' Art Studio

4. Ace of Spades Cocktails
5. C. and L. Market

Indexing Order

Unit 1	Unit 2	Unit 3	Unit 4	Unit 5
1. X	Y	Z	Blouse	Company (The)
2. Smiley	Joseph	Lock	Company (The)	
3. Harris'	Liz	Art	Studio	
4. Ace (of)	Spades	Cocktails		
5. C. (and)	L.	Market		

Alphabetic Order

Ace (of) Spades Cocktails
C. (and) L. Market
Harris', Liz, Art Studio
Smiley, Joseph, Lock Co. (The)
XYZ Blouse Co. (The)

Practice 1: Index the unarranged names below. Then place them in alphabetic order.

Unarranged Names

1. The Lila Harris Corp.
2. H. B. L. Caterers
3. Bill & Lil's Steak House

4. Bar K Ranch
5. E-Z Laundry Co.

Indexing Order

Unit 1	Unit 2	Unit 3	Unit 4	Unit 5
1. ___	___	___	___	___
2. ___	___	___	___	___
3. ___	___	___	___	___
4. ___	___	___	___	___
5. ___	___	___	___	___

Alphabetic Order

_____

_____

_____

_____

_____

A common business name that has abbreviations is a radio or television station. The call letters of the radio or television station are treated in the same way as in any other business name — each letter is a separate indexing unit. Then the words *Radio Station* or *Television Station* are indexed next.

Some companies doing business with several radio or television stations might index these names first by the title *Radio Station* or *Television Station*, then by the call letters to keep these business names in one place in the file.

The unarranged names below have been indexed and then placed in alphabetic order in the list below.

Unarranged Names

KNOW Radio Station
KTM Television Station
KRN Associates

Indexing Order

Unit 1	Unit 2	Unit 3	Unit 4	Unit 5	Unit 6
K	N	O	W	Radio	Station
K	T	M	Television	Station	
K	R	N	Associates		

Alphabetic Order

KAM Superette
KNOW Radio Station
K (&) P Truck Repair Service
KRN Associates
KTD, Inc.
KTM Television Station
Kenwood Motor Home Sales
Kyle('s) Soda Shop

Index the unarranged names below. Then place them in alphabetic order in the list on the right.

Unarranged Names

S E C, Inc.
Wm. Siefert Taxi Company

Indexing Order

Unit 1	Unit 2	Unit 3	Unit 4	Alphabetic Order
_____	_____	_____	_____	S (&) H Candies, Inc.
_____	_____	_____	_____	Shore Travel Agency
				Shorter, Pat, (&) Sons
				Simms, B. (&) L., Cleaners

When the titles *Mr.*, *Miss*, *Mrs.*, and *Ms.* are used in business names, they are indexed as written. Other titles, such as *Dr.* and *Prof.*, are indexed as though they were spelled in full.

Some of the names below are *not* in correct indexing order. If a name is in *correct* indexing order, a check mark has been placed in the *Right* column. If a name is *not* in correct indexing order, a check mark has been placed in the *Wrong* column. Then each incorrectly indexed name has been written in *correct* indexing order below.

		Indexing Order			**Answers**	
Unarranged Names	**Unit 1**	**Unit 2**	**Unit 3**	**Unit 4**	**Right**	**Wrong**
Ms. Liz's Designer Jeans	Liz('s)	Designer	Jeans (Ms.)			√
Mr. Dino's	Mister	Dino('s)				√
Mister New Yorker Stores	Mister	New	Yorker	Stores	√	
Mr. & Mrs. Clothing Store	Mr. (&)	Mrs.	Clothing	Store	√	
Designs by Miss Lane	Designs (by)	Lane (Miss)				√
Prof. Brown's Rock Shop	Professor	Brown('s)	Rock	Shop	√	
Dr. Pepper Bottling Co.	Dr.	Pepper	Bottling	Company		√

Corrected Indexing Order

Unit 1	Unit 2	Unit 3	Unit 4
Ms.	Liz('s)	Designer	Jeans
Mr.	Dino('s)		
Designs (by)	Miss	Lane	
Doctor	Pepper	Bottling	Company

Practice 3: Some of the names below are *not* in correct indexing order. If a name is in *correct* indexing order, place a check mark in the *Right* column. If a name is *not* in correct indexing order, place a check mark in the *Wrong* column. Then write each incorrectly indexed name in *correct* indexing order below.

Unarranged Names	Indexing Order Unit 1	Unit 2	Unit 3	Unit 4	Answers Right	Wrong
Mr. Clean's Janitors	Clean('s)	Janitors (Mr.)			1. _____	_____
Ms. Flowers	Ms.	Flowers			2. _____	_____
Dr. J's Pet Clinic	Doctor	J('s)	Pet	Clinic	3. _____	_____
Mrs. Evans' Beauty Shops	Evans' (Mrs.)	Beauty	Shops		4. _____	_____
Professor Joe's Books	Professor	Joe('s)	Books		5. _____	_____
The Doctor's Clinic	The	Doctor's	Clinic		6. _____	_____
Miss Sue Sporting Shop	Miss	Sue	Sporting	Shop	7. _____	_____

Corrected Indexing Order

Unit 1	Unit 2	Unit 3	Unit 4
_____	_____	_____	_____
_____	_____	_____	_____
_____	_____	_____	_____
_____	_____	_____	_____
_____	_____	_____	_____

The unarranged names below have been coded and placed in alphabetic order.

Unarranged Names	Alphabetic Order
2 3 1 4 Robt. J. Parton Industries	Big Red Q Printing
1 2 3 4 C (&) B Industries, Inc.	C (&) B Industries, Inc.
1 2 3 4 Big Red Q Printing	Goetz('s) TV Repair
1 2 3 4 Granny('s) Ice Cream Shop	Granny('s) Ice Cream Shop
1 2 3 *Goetz('s) TV (Television) Repair	Parton, Robert J., Industries
1 2 3 4 5 WKO Radio Station	WKO Radio Station

*Another way to code the familiar abbreviation *TV* is to code it as two separate units and not as the complete word *Television*. *T* would be Unit 2, and *V* would be Unit 3.

Practice 4: Code the unarranged names below. Then place them in alphabetic order.

Unarranged Names	Alphabetic Order
T K F, Inc.	_____
WLWT Television Station	_____
Pat Tarrant Travel Agency	_____
O K Tire Store	_____
Mister Magoo Bar & Grill	_____

Integrated Practice J: Code the unarranged names below and then put them in alphabetic order.

Unarranged Names	Alphabetic Order
Thos. Crown & Sons	_____
T. J. Counts Draperies	_____
T J Drug Co.	_____
Thomas & Conte Drapes, Inc.	_____
Ms. Thomas' Drapery Corp.	_____
C & T Decorators, Inc.	_____
Prof. Thomas, Inc.	_____
Geo. Draper & Son, Inc.	_____
KARK Television Station	_____
Adela Colon Hardware Co.	_____

WHAT HAVE YOU LEARNED IN SECTION 1?

(1) A business name may contain a person's abbreviated (shortened) first name. When this occurs, a period is usually placed at the end of the abbreviation.

(2) To index an abbreviated personal name in a business name, write it out in full. When you alphabetize this type of name, _think_ of the name as being spelled out in full.

(3) When the brief form of a first name (Don, Pat, etc.) is used, the brief form is indexed as it is spelled.

(4) When a business name uses letters of the alphabet as part of the name, each letter is indexed as a separate indexing unit in the order in which it is shown in the name.

(5) When the titles _Mr._, _Miss_, _Mrs._, and _Ms._ are used in business names, they are indexed as written. Other titles, such as _Dr._ and _Prof._, are indexed as though they were spelled in full.

(6) _TV_ may be either indexed as two separate units or spelled in full — _television_ — and indexed as one unit.

SECTION 2   BUSINESS NAMES WITH NUMBERS

You have seen that business firms use names of people as well as special names. A special name may be one with just letters of the alphabet as part of the company name. Special names are used because it is easier for customers to remember unusual names. This may mean more business for the company.

Another kind of unusual business name is one that includes numbers. Here are some examples:

8th Avenue Garage   The 500 Building

51st Street Market   Thirty-fifth Street Outlet Store

The 72 Club

/

As you can see, a business may use any number it wishes as part of its name. The number may be spelled out (Thirty-Fifth Street Outlet Store) or it may be written in regular number form (The 72 Club).

To index a number in a business name, spell out the number and consider it as *one* indexing unit. By spelling out a number in a business name, a number can be easily compared and alphabetized with other business names.

E(+)H Diner

Eighth Avenue Garage

Ernest, Beth, Antiques

You are now ready to index business names with numbers. Here are a few points you should remember:

(1) Numbers are indexed in the order in which they are written in the company name.

(2) No matter how large the number may be, it is always spelled out and indexed as *one* unit.

(3) Four-digit numbers are spelled out in hundreds (2019 is written as twenty hundred nineteen). Larger numbers are spelled out in thousands, ten thousands, etc.

Notice how the unarranged business names illustrated on page 99 have been indexed in alphabetic order below.

Indexing Order

Arranged Names	Unit 1	Unit 2	Unit 3	Unit 4
8th Avenue Garage	Eighth	Avenue	Garage	
51st Street Market	Fifty-first	Street	Market	
The 500 Building	Five hundred	Building (The)		
The 72 Club	Seventy-two	Club (The)		
Thirty-Fifth Street Outlet Store	Thirty-Fifth	Street	Outlet	Store

The unarranged names below have been indexed and placed in alphabetic order.

Unarranged Names

1. 18th and Main Street News
2. Second Avenue Shoes, Inc.
3. The 130th Street Hat Shop
4. 10¢ Toy Shop

Indexing Order

Unit 1	Unit 2	Unit 3	Unit 4	Alphabetic Order
1. Eighteenth (and)	Main	Street	News	18th (and) Main Street News
2. Second	Avenue	Shoes	Incorporated	130th Street Hat Shop (The)
3. One hundred thirtieth	Street	Hat	Shop (The)	Second Avenue Shoes, Inc.
4. Ten	Cent	Toy	Shop	10¢ Toy Shop

Practice 1: Index the unarranged names below and then place them in alphabetic order.

Unarranged Names

1. 1900 Pacific Apartments
2. Pieces of Eight Club
3. $5 Daily Rentals
4. 21st Century Shop

Indexing Order

Unit 1	Unit 2	Unit 3	Unit 4	Alphabetic Order
1. _____	_____	_____	_____	_____
2. _____	_____	_____	_____	_____
3. _____	_____	_____	_____	_____
4. _____	_____	_____	_____	_____

The unarranged names below have been indexed. If the indexing order is *correct*, a check mark has been placed in the *Right* column. If the indexing order is *not* correct, a check mark has been placed in the *Wrong* column.

Unarranged Names	Unit 1	Indexing Order Unit 2	Unit 3	Unit 4		Answers Right	Wrong
Tenth Avenue Stores, Inc.	Tenth	Avenue	Stores	Incorporated	1.	✓	
4th Street Furriers	4th Street	Furriers			2.		✓
Fifteen Mile Motel	Fifteen	Mile	Motel		3.	✓	

Practice 2: The unarranged names below have been indexed. If the indexing order is *correct*, place a check mark in the *Right* column. If the indexing order is *not* correct, place a check mark in the *Wrong* column.

Unarranged Names	Unit 1	Indexing Order Unit 2	Unit 3	Unit 4		Answers Right	Wrong
9th Avenue Drugs, Inc.	Ninth	Avenue	Drugs	Incorporated	1.		
A-1 Auto Club	A-	1	Auto	Club	2.		
Three A Associates	Three	A	Associates		3.		
Harry's 16 Shop	Sixteen	Harry('s)	Shop		4.		

The unarranged names below have been indexed. Then they have been placed in alphabetic order in the list on the right.

Unarranged Names

1. 88 Music Corp.
2. Sweet 16 Candies

Unit 1	Indexing Order Unit 2	Unit 3	Alphabetic Order
1. Eighty-eight	Music	Corporation	*88 Music Corp.*
			92nd Street Theater
2. Sweet	Sixteen	Candies	Sentry Chewing Gum Company
			7-11 Food Mart
			Sunshine Swimwear, Inc.
			Sweet 16 Candies

Practice 3: Index the unarranged names below. Then place them in alphabetic order in the list on the right.

Unarranged Names

1. 58th Avenue Barber Shop
2. The Four Seasons Hotel

Indexing Order

	Unit 1	Unit 2	Unit 3	Unit 4	Alphabetic Order
1.	_____	_____	_____	_____	
					Famous Shoe Stores
2.	_____	_____	_____	_____	
					Favorite Men('s) Shops
					Fina Surveying Equipment Co.
					Fulcrum Watch Corp.
					_____

You are now ready to "straighten out" the files. One of the names below has been placed in *incorrect* alphabetic order because it was indexed incorrectly. The name that is *not* in correct alphabetic order has been crossed out. Then it has been written in correct indexing order and placed in correct alphabetic order.

Unarranged Names

Cloud Nine Mattress Co.   First Street Repair Shops
Sal's Fine Jewelry, Inc.   32nd Street Clothing Store

Corrected Indexing Order

Unit 1	Unit 2	Unit 3	Unit 4	Alphabetic Order
Sal('s)	*Fine*	*Jewelry*	*Incorporated*	
				Cloud Nine Mattress Co.
				~~Fine Jewelry, Sal('s), Inc.~~
				First Street Repair Shops
				Sal('s) Fine Jewelry, Inc.
				32nd Street Clothing Store

Practice 4: "Straighten out" the files below. One of the names has been placed in *incorrect* alphabetic order because it was indexed incorrectly. Cross out the name that is *not* in correct alphabetic order. Then write that name in correct indexing order and place it in correct alphabetic order.

Unarranged Names

10th Avenue Fruit Stores
Theodore & Jack, Inc.
20th Street Jewelers, Inc.

Theo. Jacks & Sons, Inc.
24-Hour Cleaners

Corrected Indexing Order

Unit 1	Unit 2	Unit 3	Unit 4	Alphabetic Order
_____	_____	_____	_____	10th Avenue Fruit Stores
				Theodore (&) Jack, Inc.
				Theo. Jacks (&) Sons, Inc.
				20th Street Jewelers, Inc.
				24-Hour Cleaners

Some of the names below are *not* in correct indexing order. If a name is in *correct* indexing order, a check mark has been placed in the *Right* column. If a name is *not* in correct indexing order, a check mark has been placed in the *Wrong* column. Then each incorrectly indexed name has been written in correct indexing order below.

Unarranged Names	Unit 1	Unit 2	Unit 3	Unit 4	Right	Wrong
		Indexing Order			**Answers**	
7th Avenue Stores, Inc.	Seventh	Avenue	Stores	Incorporated	✓	
55th Street Garage	Fifty	fifth	Street	Garage		✓
33rd Street Tailors	Thirty-	third	Street	Tailors		✓
The 25 Dress Shop	The	Twenty-five	Dress	Shop		✓

Corrected Indexing Order

Unit 1	Unit 2	Unit 3
Fifty-fifth	Street	Garage
Thirty-third	Street	Tailors
Twenty-five	Dress	Shop (The)

Practice 5: Some of the names below are *not* in correct indexing order. If a name is in *correct* indexing order, place a check mark in the *Right* column. If a name is *not* in correct indexing order, place a check mark in the *Wrong* column. Then write each incorrectly indexed name in correct indexing order below.

| Unarranged Names | Indexing Order | | | | Answers | |
	Unit 1	Unit 2	Unit 3	Unit 4	Right	Wrong
105 Building Co.	One hundred	Five	Building	Co.	1. _____	_____
3rd Street Camera Shop	Third	Street	Camera	Shop	2. _____	_____
The 502 Corp.	The	502	Corporation		3. _____	_____
The 8th Club, Inc.	Eighth	Club	Incorporated	(The)	4. _____	_____

Corrected Indexing Order

Unit 1	Unit 2	Unit 3	Unit 4
_____	_____	_____	_____
_____	_____	_____	_____
_____	_____	_____	_____
_____	_____	_____	_____

Integrated Practice K: Code the unarranged names below and then put them in alphabetic order.

Unarranged Names	Alphabetic Order
52 Madison Avenue	_____
F. Fuentes & Son, Inc.	_____
Francis' Barber Shop	_____
Frieda Fulton & Sons, Furriers	_____
501 Main Street Corp.	_____
Fisher Pump & Equipment Co.	_____
FM Floor Coverings	_____
Chas. Felix & Sons, Inc.	_____

WHAT HAVE YOU LEARNED IN SECTION 2?

(1) A business firm may use a number as part of its name.
(2) The number may be spelled out (such as <u>fifty-two</u>) or written in regular number form (such as <u>52</u>).
(3) When a number is indexed it is always spelled out and counted as one unit, no matter how long it may be.
(4) Four-digit numbers are spelled out in hundreds (<u>6666</u> is written as <u>sixty-six hundred sixty-six</u>). Larger numbers are spelled out in thousands, ten thousands, etc.
(5) When putting business names that contain numbers in alphabetic order, think of the number as being spelled out, even though it may not be written that way.

SECTION 3   BUSINESS NAMES THAT CAN BE WRITTEN AS ONE OR TWO WORDS

Some business firms have names using words that may be written as one or two words. Here are some examples:

Inter City Trading Corp.   Northwest Industries
South Western Coal Co.   Tri-County Oil Deliveries, Inc.

Words that may be written as one or two words are indexed as one unit. Hyphens are disregarded.

Examples of words that are sometimes separated into two words are *airlines, airport, carload, crossroads, downtown, eastside, goodwill, halfway, railroad*, and points of the compass such as *northeast, northwest, southeast*, and *southwest*.

Many words that may be written as one or two words have prefixes. Examples of common prefixes are *anti-, bi-, co-, inter-, mid-, mini-, non-, trans-*, and *tri-*.

An up-to-date dictionary should be used to determine if a word written as two words should be indexed as only one word. For example, *drugstore* and *bookstore* are shown as one word in the dictionary and should be indexed as one unit even when written as two words in a business name.

The business names illustrated above would be indexed as follows:

	Indexing Order			
Unarranged Names	**Unit 1**	**Unit 2**	**Unit 3**	**Unit 4**
Inter City Trading Corp.	Inter City	Trading	Corporation	
South Western Coal Co.	South Western	Coal	Company	
Northwest Industries	Northwest	Industries		
Tri-County Oil Deliveries, Inc.	Tri-County	Oil	Deliveries	Incorporated

The business names below have been indexed in alphabetic order.

	Indexing Order			
Arranged Names	**Unit 1**	**Unit 2**	**Unit 3**	**Unit 4**
A-One Answering Service	A-	One	Answering	Service
Bi-Monthly News Service	Bi-Monthly	News	Service	
Mid West Air Lines, Inc.	Mid West	Air Lines	Incorporated	
Nation Wide Moving Co.	Nation Wide	Moving	Company	
North West Auto Rentals	North West	Auto	Rentals	
Sav-Co Mini-Mart	Sav-	Co	Mini-Mart	
Save-Way Discount Drugstore	Save-	Way	Discount	Drugstore
Southwestern Transit Co.	Southwestern	Transit	Company	
Transworld Corporation	Transworld	Corporation		
Tri-State Auto & Truck Sales	Tri-State	Auto (&)	Truck	Sales

The unarranged names below have been indexed. Then they have been placed in alphabetic order in the list below.

		Indexing Order	
Unarranged Names	**Unit 1**	**Unit 2**	**Unit 3**
Mid Western Trucking Co.	Mid Western	Trucking	Company
Inter City Rentals, Inc.	Inter City	Rentals	Incorporated

Alphabetic Order

Ingram (&) Peters, Inc.

Inter City Rentals, Inc.

Interstate Car Rentals, Inc.

Mid Western Trucking Co.

Southard (&) Sons, Inc.

Practice 1: Index the unarranged names below. Then place them in alphabetic order in the list below.

		Indexing Order		
Unarranged Names	**Unit 1**	**Unit 2**	**Unit 3**	**Unit 4**
Southern Gas Co.	_____	_____	_____	_____
North West Fisheries, Inc.	_____	_____	_____	_____
Inter-City Truckers, Inc.	_____	_____	_____	_____

Alphabetic Order

Ingalls, North (&) Company

Interrano (&) Perez, Inc.

North, C. J., (&) Co.

South (&) South, Inc.

South-East Industries, Inc.

You are now ready to "straighten out" the files. One of the names below has been placed in *incorrect* alphabetic order because it was indexed incorrectly. The name that is *not* in correct alphabetic order has been crossed out and then placed in correct indexing order. Then it has been written in correct alphabetic order.

Unarranged Names

Eastern Freight Deliveries	17th Street Shopping Mart
South-Eastern Tours, Inc.	South-East Taxi Service, Inc.

Corrected Indexing Order

Unit 1	Unit 2	Unit 3	Unit 4	Alphabetic Order
South-East	*Taxi*	*Service*	*Incorporated*	
				Eastern Freight Deliveries
				17th Street Shopping Mart
				South-East Taxi Service, Inc.
				South-Eastern Tours, Inc.
				~~Taxi Service, Inc., South-East~~

Practice 2: "Straighten out" the files below. One of the names has been placed in *incorrect* alphabetic order because it was indexed incorrectly. Cross out the name that is *not* in correct alphabetic order. Then write that name in *correct* indexing order and place it in correct alphabetic order.

Unarranged Names

North-South Liquor Store	North Eastern Air Terminals, Inc.
Northeast Railway Corp.	91st Avenue Drug Store

Corrected Indexing Order

Unit 1	Unit 2	Unit 3	Unit 4	Alphabetic Order
_____	_____	_____	_____	
				91st Avenue Drug Store
				Northeast Railway Corp.
				North Eastern Air Terminals, Inc.
				North-South Liquor Store

Code the unarranged names below and then put them in alphabetic order.

Unarranged Names	Alphabetic Order
16th Street Hardware Store	_____
South-Eastern Hardware Co.	_____
E Z Cleaners	_____
E. Evans & Sons, Inc.	_____
Interstate Fruit Stores	_____
I & E Electrical Corp.	_____
ICU Services	_____
Ira West & Sons, Inc.	_____
Inter-City Food Stores	_____
South-Western Fuel Co.	_____

WHAT HAVE YOU LEARNED IN SECTION 3?	(1) A business name may use a word that is usually spelled as one word but have it written as two words (such as <u>North East</u>). It may also use a hyphen (-) to divide it into two words (such as <u>North-East</u>). (2) A word such as <u>North-East</u> that is shown as two words or with a hyphen is still indexed as one unit. (3) Alphabetize such names as if they were one unit.

SECTION 4   SIMPLE AND COMPOUND GEOGRAPHIC NAMES

Many businesses use names of places (geographic names) in their company names. Here are some examples:

Albany Transit Co.   Vermont Trading Corp.
Dallas Drugstores, Inc.   Portland Discount Stores, Inc.

As you can see, a geographic name can be that of a *state, city,* or *town.* There is no special problem in indexing and alphabetizing such names. Each geographic name is a separate unit and is counted in the order in which it appears in the company name. The names above would be indexed and alphabetized as shown below:

	Indexing Order			
Unarranged Names	**Unit 1**	**Unit 2**	**Unit 3**	**Unit 4**
Albany Transit Co.	Albany	Transit	Company	
Vermont Trading Corp.	Vermont	Trading	Corporation	
Dallas Drugstores, Inc.	Dallas	Drugstores	Incorporated	
Portland Discount Stores, Inc.	Portland	Discount	Stores	Incorporated

Alphabetic Order

Albany Transit Co.
Dallas Drugstores, Inc.
Portland Discount Stores, Inc.
Vermont Trading Corp.

Some geographic names (places) have two parts, such as:

Corpus Christi Sales Corp.   South Dakota Bus Co.
New Mexico Textiles, Inc.   South Bend Insurance Agency

Names like the ones above are called *compound names.* They have more than one part. When you index and alphabetize compound names, count each part of the name as a separate unit and put it in the order in which it appears in the name.

Notice in the example below how the compound names are indexed and then placed in alphabetic order.

Indexing Order

Unarranged Names	Unit 1	Unit 2	Unit 3	Unit 4
Corpus Christi Sales Corp.	Corpus	Christi	Sales	Corporation
New Mexico Textiles, Inc.	New	Mexico	Textiles	Incorporated
South Dakota Bus Co.	South	Dakota	Bus	Company
South Bend Insurance Agency	South	Bend	Insurance	Agency

Alphabetic Order

Corpus Christi Sales Corp.
New Mexico Textiles, Inc.
South Bend Insurance Agency
South Dakota Bus Co.

Many compound names of places in the United States consist of foreign words. Here are some examples of such names used as parts of business names.

San Francisco Mining Co.
Rio Grande Meat Corp.
Terre Haute Plumbers
San Diego Tours, Inc.

With most geographic names containing foreign words, each part is counted as a separate indexing unit. Here is the way the names above would be indexed:

Indexing Order

Unarranged Names	Unit 1	Unit 2	Unit 3	Unit 4
San Francisco Mining Co.	San	Francisco	Mining	Company
Rio Grande Meat Corp.	Rio	Grande	Meat	Corporation
Terre Haute Plumbers	Terre	Haute	Plumbers	
San Diego Tours, Inc.	San	Diego	Tours	Incorporated

Some compound geographic names use foreign words which mean *the* or *of the*. Some of the more common foreign words which mean *the* or *of the* are: *el, los, la, las, del,* and *des.* Here are some examples of compound geographic names that use these words as part of a business name.

Los Angeles Water Co.
El Paso Oil + Gas, Inc.
Des Moines Drilling Corp.
Las Vegas Motor Inn, Inc.

Foreign words meaning *the* or *of the* are counted with the word following them as one indexing unit. Here is the way the names above would be indexed:

	Indexing Order			
Unarranged Names	**Unit 1**	**Unit 2**	**Unit 3**	**Unit 4**
Los Angeles Water Co.	Los Angeles	Water	Company	
El Paso Oil & Gas, Inc.	El Paso	Oil (&)	Gas	Incorporated
Des Moines Drilling Corp.	Des Moines	Drilling	Corporation	
Las Vegas Motor Inn, Inc.	Las Vegas	Motor	Inn	Incorporated

Some compound geographic names containing the word *St.* or *Ste.*, meaning Saint or Sainte, are used as part of a business name. Here are two examples of such names:

St. Paul Barber Supplies
St. Petersburg Tourist Co.

The abbreviation *St.* or *Ste.* is spelled out when indexing and is counted as a separate indexing unit. Here is the way the names above would be indexed:

	Indexing Order			
Unarranged Names	**Unit 1**	**Unit 2**	**Unit 3**	**Unit 4**
St. Paul Barber Supplies	Saint	Paul	Barber	Supplies
St. Petersburg Tourist Co.	Saint	Petersburg	Tourist	Company

You are now ready to index and alphabetize the different types of geographic names. The unarranged business names containing geographic names below have been indexed and placed in alphabetic order.

	Indexing Order				
Unarranged Names	**Unit 1**	**Unit 2**	**Unit 3**	**Unit 4**	**Alphabetic Order**
New Jersey Hat Shops	New	Jersey	Hat	Shops	El Paso Fuel Co.
El Paso Fuel Co.	El Paso	Fuel	Company		New Jersey Hat Shops
St. Joseph Food Stores	Saint	Joseph	Food	Stores	St. Joseph Food Stores

Practice 1: Index the unarranged names below. Then place them in alphabetic order.

Unarranged Names	Indexing Order			
	Unit 1	**Unit 2**	**Unit 3**	**Unit 4**
Los Alamos Pottery Shop	_____	_____	_____	_____
New Orleans Beverage Co.	_____	_____	_____	_____
Newtown Dry Cleaning Co.	_____	_____	_____	_____
St. Albans Fruit Co.	_____	_____	_____	_____

Alphabetic Order

_____

_____

_____

_____

The unarranged names below have been indexed and then placed in alphabetic order in the list below.

Unarranged Names	Indexing Order			
	Unit 1	**Unit 2**	**Unit 3**	**Unit 4**
St. Louis Mfg. Corp.	Saint	Louis	Manufacturing	Corporation
San Francisco Realty Corp.	San	Francisco	Realty	Corporation

Alphabetic Order

_____

Sachs Fur Co. (The)

_____

Sacramento Theater Corporation

St. Louis Mfg. Corp.

Sainte, Evelyn (&) Sons, Inc.

San Francisco Realty Corp.

Santos (&) Sons, Inc.

_____

Sanzone, Alvin, Fur Co.

_____

Practice 2: Index the unarranged names below. Then place them in alphabetic order in the list below.

Indexing Order

Unarranged Names	Unit 1	Unit 2	Unit 3	Unit 4
New England Investment Co.	_____	_____	_____	_____
Newton Foundries, Inc.	_____	_____	_____	_____

Alphabetic Order

National Tie Company
_____

New York Sales Company
_____

Newman (&) Santiago, Inc.
_____

Newtown Lumber Co.
_____

Norris, Ellen, Boutique
_____

Some of the names below are *not* in correct indexing order. If a name is in *correct* indexing order, a check mark has been placed in the *Right* column. If a name is *not* in correct indexing order, a check mark has been placed in the *Wrong* column. Then the name has been written in correct indexing order below.

	Indexing Order				Answers	
Unarranged Names	Unit 1	Unit 2	Unit 3	Unit 4	Right	Wrong
New Rochelle Light Co.	New Rochelle	Light	Company		_____	✓
St. Joseph Glove Co.	Saint	Joseph	Glove	Company	✓	_____
El Paso Gas & Electric Co.	El Paso	Gas (&)	Electric	Company	✓	_____
New Haven Upholstery Co.	New Haven	Upholstery	Company		_____	✓
Newport Boat Co.	New	Port	Boat	Company	_____	✓

Corrected Indexing Order

Unit 1	Unit 2	Unit 3	Unit 4
New	Rochelle	Light	Company
New	Haven	Upholstery	Company
Newport	Boat	Company	

Practice 3: Some of the names below are *not* in correct indexing order. If a name is in *correct* indexing order, place a check mark in the *Right* column. If a name is *not* in correct indexing order, place a check mark in the *Wrong* column. Then write the name in correct indexing order below.

| | | Indexing Order | | | | Answers | |
Unarranged Names	Unit 1	Unit 2	Unit 3	Unit 4		Right	Wrong
South Orange Truckers, Inc.	South	Orange	Truckers	Incorporated	1. _____	_____
El Paso Printers, Inc.	El	Paso	Printers	Incorporated	2. _____	_____
Fort Worth Auto Corp.	Fort	Worth	Auto	Corporation	3. _____	_____
Mount Vernon Cleaners Co.	Mount Vernon	Cleaners	Company		4. _____	_____
San Jose Tool Co.	San	Jose	Tool	Company	5. _____	_____

Corrected Indexing Order

Unit 1	Unit 2	Unit 3	Unit 4
_____	_____	_____	_____
_____	_____	_____	_____
_____	_____	_____	_____
_____	_____	_____	_____
_____	_____	_____	_____

You are now ready to "straighten out" the files. One of the names below has been placed in *incorrect* alphabetic order because it was indexed incorrectly. Notice that the name that is *not* in correct alphabetic order has been crossed out and written in correct indexing order. Then it has been placed in correct alphabetic order below.

| | **Corrected Indexing Order** | | |
Unarranged Names	Unit 1	Unit 2	Unit 3	Unit 4
St. Augustine Shirt Co.	*Saint*	*Augustine*	*Shirt*	*Company*
Santana & Sons, Jewelers	_____	_____	_____	_____
Salem Hats, Inc.	_____	_____	_____	_____

Alphabetic Order

St. Augustine Shirt Co.

Salem Hats, Inc.

_____

Santana (&) Sons, Jewelers

_____

~~St. Augustine Shirt Co.~~

_____

Practice 4: "Straighten out" the files below. One of the names has been placed in *incorrect* alphabetic order because it was indexed incorrectly. Cross out the name that is *not* in correct alphabetic order. Then write that name in *correct* indexing order and place it in correct alphabetic order.

Unarranged Names	Corrected Indexing Order			
	Unit 1	Unit 2	Unit 3	Unit 4
Elkins Dairy Stores	_____	_____	_____	_____
E. Esteva & Guzman, Inc.	_____	_____	_____	_____
El Paso Lamp Co.	_____	_____	_____	_____

Alphabetic Order

_____

E. Esteva (&) Guzman, Inc.

_____

Elkins Dairy Stores

_____

El Paso Lamp Co.

_____

The unarranged names below have been indexed and then placed in alphabetic order in the list of names below.

Unarranged Names	Indexing Order			
	Unit 1	Unit 2	Unit 3	Unit 4
Long Island Adventure Tours	Long	Island	Adventure	Tours
St. Louis Grayson Hotel	Saint	Louis	Grayson	Hotel
Los Altos Laundry Co.	Los Altos	Laundry	Company	

Alphabetic Order

_____

Lexington Car Corp.

Long Island Adventure Tours

Lorraine Fashions, Inc.

Los Altos Laundry Co.

Sable Coats, Inc.

St. Louis Grayson Hotel

Sandoval('s) Delicatessen, Inc.

_____

Practice 5: Index the unarranged names below. Then place them in alphabetic order in the list below.

	Indexing Order		
Unarranged Names	**Unit 1**	**Unit 2**	**Unit 3**
N and O Supermarkets	_____	_____	_____
North East Motel	_____	_____	_____
Nantucket Roadside Hotels	_____	_____	_____

Alphabetic Order

_____

Nanking Chinese Foods, Inc.

_____

Nassau Travelers Insurance Corp.

_____

New City Realty Corporation

_____

Integrated Practice M: Code the unarranged names below and then put them in alphabetic order.

Unarranged Names	**Alphabetic Order**
St. Louis Dental Laboratories	_____
Los Angeles Trading Corp.	_____
Santos' Hats, Inc.	_____
Ste. Agathe Importing Co.	_____
Sainto & Louis, Inc.	_____
J. L. Lomax Deliveries	_____
SAC Corp.	_____
Santos the Baker, Inc.	_____

WHAT HAVE YOU LEARNED IN SECTION 4?

(1) A business may use a geographic name as part of its name.
(2) A geographic name may be simple or compound. A simple geographic name has one part and is indexed as one unit. A compound geographic name has more than one part. The parts are indexed as two units, in the order in which they are written.
(3) The word Saint or Sainte is indexed as a separate unit even if it is abbreviated to St. or Ste.
(4) Foreign words meaning the or of the are counted with the word following them as one indexing unit.

SECTION 5   SIMULATED OFFICE PROBLEMS

Many letters and reports in business offices today are stored on *magnetic cards*, or "mag cards." A mag card is a flexible plastic card on which several business letters can be filed or stored. Mag cards are about the same size and shape as the IBM computer cards which you learned to file in Part 3.

Mag cards are used by office workers who operate *word processing equipment*.

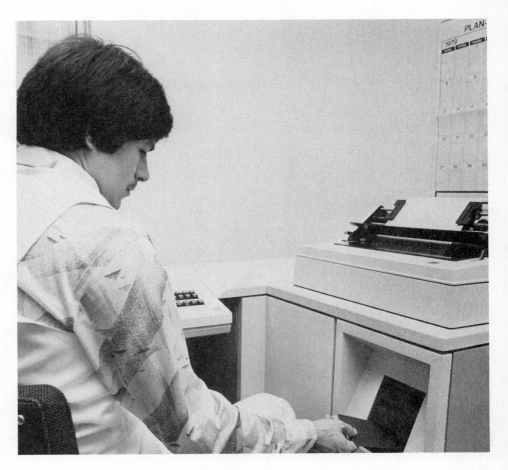

When you file or retrieve mag cards, you must be careful not to touch the card except on the label. Finger smudges, dirt, and dust will damage the information stored on the mag card just as smudges, dirt, and dust will damage your stereo records. For this reason mag cards are usually filed in a protective folder.

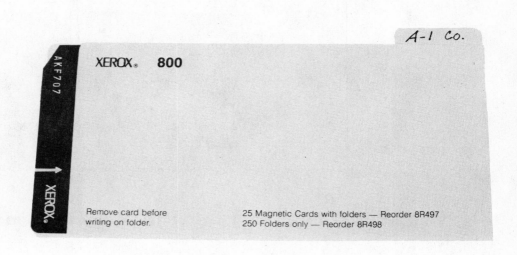

The mag cards, in their folders, are then placed in alphabetic order in a file box. Most boxes have a clear plastic cover to help keep out dust.

Each of the names below has been coded. Then the names were written on the mag card folder tabs and placed in alphabetic order in the file box.

Names

$\overset{1}{\text{De}} \overset{2}{\text{Lantis}} \overset{3}{\text{Realty, Inc.}}$

$\overset{1}{\text{Des}} \overset{2}{\text{Moines}} \overset{3}{\text{Grain Corp.}}$

$\overset{1}{\text{DC}} \overset{2}{} \overset{3}{\text{Auto}} \overset{4}{\text{Rental,}} \overset{5}{\text{Inc.}}$

$\overset{2}{\text{Ernesta}} \overset{1}{\text{De}} \overset{}{\text{Salvo}} \overset{3}{\text{Co.}}$

$\overset{2}{\text{Thos.}} \overset{1}{\text{Deitz}} \overset{}{\text{(\&)}} \overset{3}{\text{Sons}}$

$\overset{2}{\text{Angela}} \overset{1}{\text{De}} \overset{}{\text{La}} \overset{}{\text{Crosse}}$

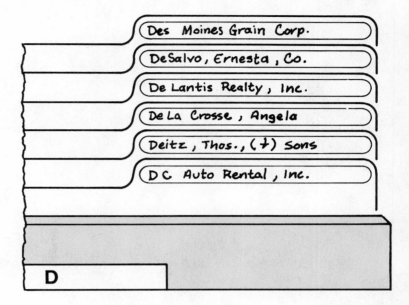

Practice 1: Mag card folders need to be prepared for the names below. Code the names. Then show how you would place the folders in the file box by writing the names in alphabetic order on the mag card folder tabs.

Names

Eighth Street Market

El Dorado Electric Co.

ESP Magic Co.

Theo. Edwards, Inc.

E-M Drapery Co.

Eastern Magic Co.

80 Club, Inc.

Alvira El Mora Co.

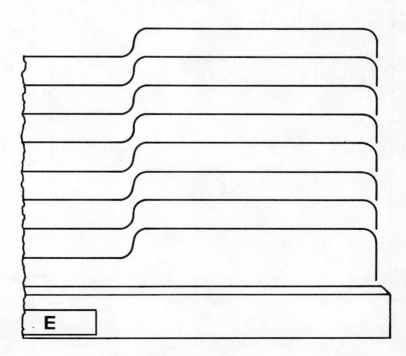

The names below have been coded. Then they have been written on the folder tab and placed in alphabetic order in the mag card file box.

Names

2   1   3
Chas. Southyn, Inc.

1   2   3   4
South Winona Canoe Co.

1 2   3   4
S-K Shipping Corp.

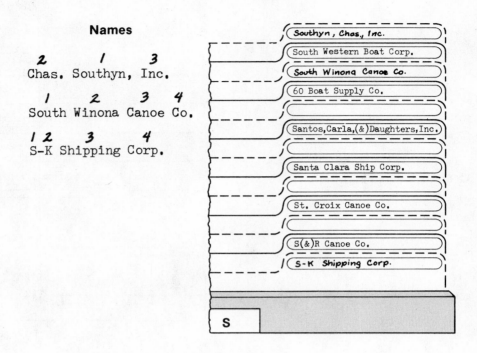

Southyn, Chas., Inc.
South Western Boat Corp.
South Winona Canoe Co.
60 Boat Supply Co.

Santos, Carla, (&) Daughters, Inc.

Santa Clara Ship Corp.

St. Croix Canoe Co.

S(&)R Canoe Co.
S-K Shipping Corp.

S

Practice 2: Code the names below. Then show how you would place them in the file box by writing the names on the correct mag card folder tabs.

Names

Lester Laseter Co.

Wilma La Garce, Inc.

Carole Losan, Inc.

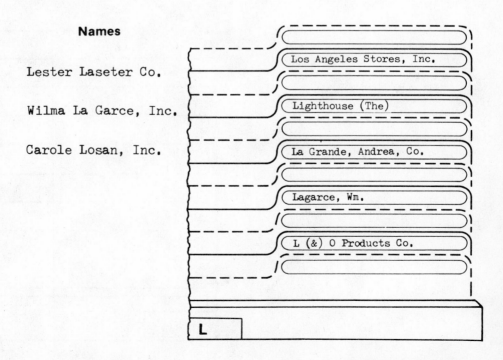

Los Angeles Stores, Inc.

Lighthouse (The)

La Grande, Andrea, Co.

Lagarce, Wm.

L (&) O Products Co.

L

Many offices use magnetic diskettes to store letters and reports. Magnetic diskettes are made of flexible plastic, like mag cards. They are about the same size and shape as 45 rpm records and are sealed in a jacket to help keep dust and dirt out.

Avery Label Systems

You must take the same care when you handle magnetic diskettes as you do when you handle mag cards. And like mag cards, magnetic diskettes are usually placed in an envelope before filing.

The envelope usually has a tab on it. In case the diskette slips out of its envelope, the name of the company is written on both the diskette label and the envelope tab.

Diskette in Envelope

File Box for Diskettes

Ring King Visibles, Inc.

Each of the diskettes below contains a report for one of the companies listed on the left. The names of the companies were first coded. Then they were written on the diskette labels in indexing order. The order in which the diskettes would be filed was shown by placing a number in the blank at the right.

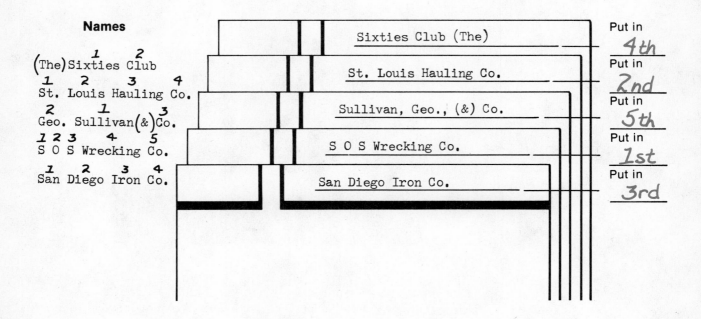

Names

           1   *2*
(The) Sixties Club
1   *2*   *3*   *4*
St. Louis Hauling Co.
  2   *1*   *3*
Geo. Sullivan (&) Co.
1 2 3   *4*   *5*
S O S Wrecking Co.
  1   *2*   *3*   *4*
San Diego Iron Co.

Sixties Club (The) — Put in 4th

St. Louis Hauling Co. — Put in 2nd

Sullivan, Geo., (&) Co. — Put in 5th

S O S Wrecking Co. — Put in 1st

San Diego Iron Co. — Put in 3rd

Practice 3: Code the names on the left. Then write the names on the diskette labels in indexing order. Show the order in which each diskette should be filed by placing a number in the blank at the right.

Names

Las Vegas Foods, Inc.

L & V Nylon Carpets, Inc.

Lee Vega & Daughters

Chas. LaVance Styling

Los Angeles Auto Co.

Put in

Put in

Put in

Put in

Put in

                                                        Part 4 ● Filing Other Business Names

Two diskettes were to be added to the files below. Notice that the names of the diskettes on the left were first coded. Then the names were written in alphabetic order on the correct blank envelope tabs in the file box.

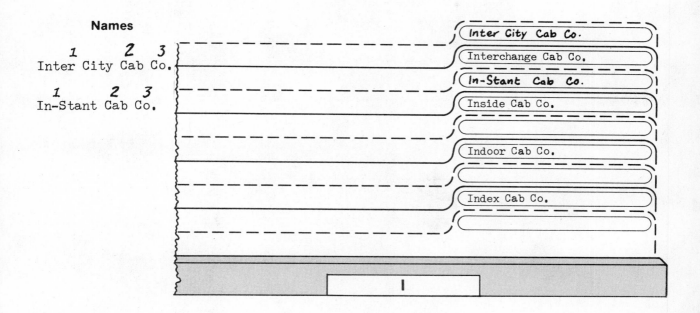

Names

1   *2* *3*
Inter City Cab Co.

1   *2* *3*
In-Stant Cab Co.

Inter City Cab Co.
Interchange Cab Co.
In-Stant Cab Co.
Inside Cab Co.

Indoor Cab Co.

Index Cab Co.

I

Practice 4: Add two diskettes to the files below. First code the names for the diskettes on the left. Then write the names in alphabetic order on the correct blank envelope tabs in the file box.

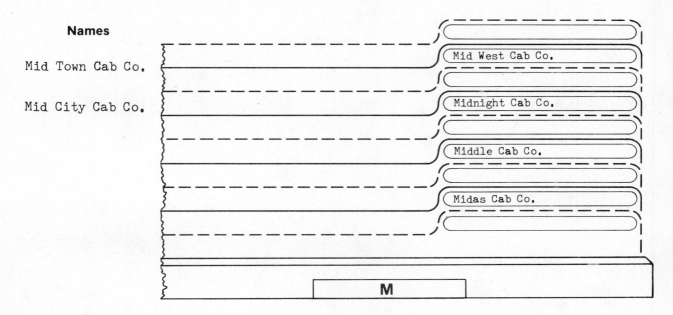

Names

Mid Town Cab Co.

Mid City Cab Co.

Mid West Cab Co.

Midnight Cab Co.

Middle Cab Co.

Midas Cab Co.

M

Two diskettes below were filed incorrectly. The two names that are not in correct alphabetic order have been crossed out and then written in correct alphabetic order.

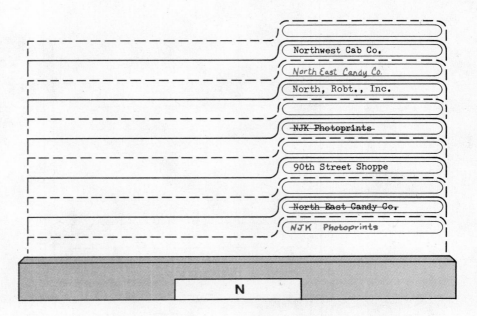

Northwest Cab Co.

North East Candy Co.

North, Robt., Inc.

~~NJK Photoprints~~

90th Street Shoppe

~~North East Candy Co.~~

NJK Photoprints

N

Practice 5: Two diskettes below have been filed incorrectly. Find the diskettes and cross out their names. Then show the correct order of the diskettes by writing the names in alphabetic order on the correct blank envelope tabs.

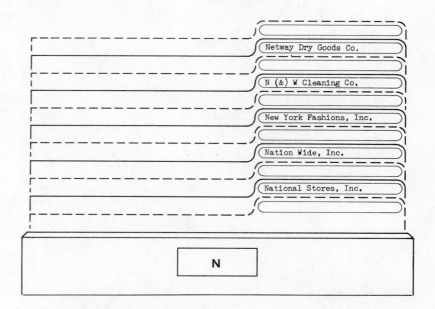

Netway Dry Goods Co.

N (&) W Cleaning Co.

New York Fashions, Inc.

Nation Wide, Inc.

National Stores, Inc.

N

PART 5

FILING GOVERNMENT, BANK, AND CHAIN STORE BUSINESS NAMES

One out of every six workers in the United States is employed by an agency of a city, county, state, or federal government. Many of those who work for government agencies are office workers.

Office positions in government are usually called *civil service* jobs. Here are some examples of beginning civil service jobs in the federal government:

GS-1   Clerk
GS-2   File Clerk
GS-6   Clerk-Typist

To get a government office job, you usually must take a *civil service examination*. Your score on this examination will be used by the government agency to help decide whether or not you will be hired for the job. You should know that many of the civil service examinations for office jobs test your ability to file the names of persons, businesses, and government units.

You have already learned how to file the names of persons and businesses. In Part 5 you will learn how to file the names of government units. For example, you will learn how to file names such as these:

The United States Department of Commerce
The Missouri Division of Family Services
The Madison County Highway Department

By learning how to file and find the names of government units, you will have a much better chance of getting an office job.

SECTION 1   U.S., LOCAL, AND FOREIGN GOVERNMENT NAMES

As you know, many government agencies handle a large number of papers that must be filed. Everyone who works has a Social Security card, and this alone means almost one hundred million names that must be filed.

In order to make it easy to file and find government names, you must realize that there are names to be filed for the U.S. government, state governments, city and town governments, and also foreign governments. You must also remember that the U.S. government has many different departments, branches, bureaus, and sections. For example, if you needed information about Social Security, you would write to the Department of Health and Human Services because Social Security is a part of that department.

U.S. Department of State
Ohio Department of Motor Vehicles
Seattle Bureau of Crime Prevention
Sweden Ministry of Agriculture

You must also realize that different levels of government (federal, state, and city) may have the same type of bureau or department. There is a Tax Division in the federal government, and there are often Tax Divisions in state and city governments as well.

All of these facts mean that you must be careful when indexing government names. The most important point to remember is that, regardless of the way in which a government name is written, the *first* unit is *always* the country, state, city, or town. Since a business firm may use the words *United States* in its name, such as *United States Steel Corp.*, use the words *United States Government* as the first three units of every federal government name. So when you index *U.S. Department of the Treasury, Department of the Treasury*, or *Department of the Treasury of the U.S.*, use the words *United States Government* as the first three units.

The U.S. Department of the Treasury would be indexed as follows:

Indexing Order

Unit 1	Unit 2	Unit 3	Unit 4	Unit 5
United	States	Government	Treasury	Department (of the)

If you are alphabetizing the names of a *state* or *city* government, the first three units would be as follows:

	Indexing Order		
Unarranged Names	**Unit 1**	**Unit 2**	**Unit 3**
New York City	New	York	City
New York State	New	York	State
Kansas State	Kansas	State	
Kansas City	Kansas	City	
Los Angeles	Los Angeles	City	

As you can see from the examples above, add the word *Government* only after *United States*.

If the word *state* or *city* is not listed in a government name, it is still added as a unit in indexing (as in *Los Angeles City*).

If you deal with the names of *foreign* governments, you may find certain words used to describe the *kind* of government, such as:

Kingdom of Sweden
Republic of France

Since the words *Kingdom* and *Republic* only describe the kind of government of these countries, use only the actual name of the country as the first indexing unit. Words that describe the kind of government (Kingdom, Republic) would then be Unit 2, as follows:

	Indexing Order		
Unarranged Names	**Unit 1**	**Unit 2**	**Unit 3**
Kingdom of Sweden	Sweden	Kingdom (of)	
Republic of France	France	Republic (of)	

Notice that the word *of* is not counted as an indexing unit.

Since you would not write to the *United States Government* or to the *Republic of France*, but to some branch or department of these governments, you must now learn how to index a *branch* or *department* of a government.

Here are some examples of branches or departments of a government:

New Jersey Department of Motor Vehicles
U.S. Department of State
Ministry of National Security, Kingdom of Sweden
Ministry of Agriculture, Republic of France
Los Angeles Department of Welfare
Dade County Police Department

When you index such names, start with the political (government geographic location — country, state, county, city, etc.) part of the name and then write the *branch* of that government. This is how you would index the names above.

Unarranged Names

1. New Jersey Dept. of Motor Vehicles
2. U.S. Dept. of State
3. Ministry of National Security, Kingdom of Sweden
4. Ministry of Agriculture, Republic of France
5. Los Angeles Dept. of Welfare
6. Dade County Police Department

Indexing Order

Unit 1	Unit 2	Unit 3	Unit 4	Unit 5	Unit 6
1. New	Jersey	State	Motor	Vehicles	Department (of)
2. United	States	Government	State	Department (of)	
3. Sweden	Kingdom (of)	National	Security	Ministry (of)	
4. France	Republic (of)	Agriculture	Ministry (of)		
5. Los Angeles	City	Welfare	Department (of)		
6. Dade	County	Police	Department		

The examples above show that:

(1) The political unit (geographic location) is always indexed first.

(2) The words *state, county*, and *city* are always written as separate indexing units, even if they do not appear in the name itself.

(3) Any words that describe a political unit, such as *Republic of*, are separate indexing units. The words *of* or *of the* are placed in parentheses.

(4) A branch of a political unit, such as the Department of Defense, is indexed *after* the political unit.

(5) Any words that describe the branch, such as *Department of*, are separate indexing units. The word *of* is disregarded. (The abbreviation for *Department, Dept.*, is spelled out when indexing.)

You are now ready to index and alphabetize names of governmental branches. The unarranged names below have been indexed and placed in alphabetic order.

Unarranged Names

1. Georgia Dept. of Banking and Finance
2. Republic of Italy, Dept. of Internal Affairs
3. St. Louis Dept. of Highways

Indexing Order

Unit 1	Unit 2	Unit 3	Unit 4	Unit 5
1. Georgia	State	Banking (and)	Finance	Department (of)
2. Italy	Republic (of)	Internal	Affairs	Department (of)
3. Saint	Louis	City	Highways	Department (of)

Alphabetic Order

Georgia, State, Banking (and) Finance, Department (of)
Italy, Republic (of), Internal Affairs, Department (of)
St. Louis, City, Highways, Department (of)

Practice 1: Index and alphabetize the names below.

Unarranged Names

1. Republic of Brazil, Ministry of Defense
2. Seattle Bureau of Crime Prevention
3. State of Alabama, Division of Public Works
4. U.S. Dept. of the Treasury

Indexing Order

Unit 1	Unit 2	Unit 3	Unit 4	Unit 5
1. ___	___	___	___	___
2. ___	___	___	___	___
3. ___	___	___	___	___
4. ___	___	___	___	___

Alphabetic Order

_____

_____

_____

_____

The unarranged names below have been indexed. If the indexing order is *correct*, a check mark has been placed in the *Right* column. If the indexing order is *not* correct, a check mark has been placed in the *Wrong* column.

Unarranged Names

1. Milwaukee Dept. of Civil Affairs
2. Colorado Bureau of Mines
3. Bureau of Civil Affairs, City of Reading

		Indexing Order				**Answers**	
Unit 1	**Unit 2**	**Unit 3**	**Unit 4**	**Unit 5**		**Right**	**Wrong**
1. Milwaukee	Affairs (Civil)	Department (of)			1.	_____	✓
2. Colorado	State	Mines	(Bureau of)		2.	_____	✓
3. Reading	City (of)	Civil	Affairs	Bureau (of)	3.	✓	_____

Practice 2: The unarranged names below have been indexed. If the indexing order is *correct*, place a check mark in the *Right* column. If the indexing order is *not* correct, place a check mark in the *Wrong* column.

Unarranged Names

1. Raleigh Dept. of Public Works
2. Fort Worth Convention Bureau
3. Division of Water Quality, State of Kentucky
4. Idaho Department of Revenue and Taxation
5. Texas Dept. of Transportation
6. Public Utilities Department, Yonkers

		Indexing Order				**Answers**	
Unit 1	**Unit 2**	**Unit 3**	**Unit 4**	**Unit 5**		**Right**	**Wrong**
1. Public	Works	Raleigh			1.	_____	_____
2. Fort	Worth	City	Convention (Bureau)		2.	_____	_____
3. Water	Quality (Div. of)	Kentucky	State		3.	_____	_____
4. Idaho	State	Revenue (and)	Taxation	Department (of)	4.	_____	_____
5. Texas	Department (of)	Transportation			5.	_____	_____
6. Yonkers	City	Public	Utilities	Department	6.	_____	_____

Now you are ready to place two government names in an alphabetic list. The unarranged names below have been indexed and placed in alphabetic order in the list of names below.

Unarranged Names

1. St. Paul Dept. of Traffic   2. U.S. Dept. of the Interior

Indexing Order

Unit 1	Unit 2	Unit 3	Unit 4	Unit 5
1. Saint	Paul	City	Traffic	Department (of)
2. United	States	Government	Interior	Department (of the)

Alphabetic Order

St. Louis, City, Health, Department (of)

St. Paul, City, Traffic, Department (of)

San Francisco, City, Sanitation, Department (of)

United States Government, Commerce, Department (of)

United States Government, Interior, Department (of the)

Practice 3: Index the unarranged names below and then place them in alphabetic order in the list of names.

Unarranged Names

1. Unionville Board of Transportation   2. U.S. Dept. of Justice

Indexing Order

Unit 1	Unit 2	Unit 3	Unit 4	Unit 5
1. _____	_____	_____	_____	_____
2. _____	_____	_____	_____	_____

Alphabetic Order

Union, City, Highways, Department (of)

United States Government, Agriculture, Department (of)

United States Government, Defense, Department (of)

The unarranged names below have been coded. Then they have been placed in alphabetic order.

Unarranged Names

    3   4   5   1   2
1. Air Control Dept. (of) Atlantic City

          2
       State
  1   3   4   5
2. Alabama   Public Works Dept.

  2   1   4   3
3. Republic (of) Austria, Dept. (of) Tourism

        2
      City
  1   4   3
4. Buffalo   Department (of) Sanitation

    1   2   3
  United States Government
      7   4   5   6
5. U.S. Department (of) Health (and) Human Services

Alphabetic Order

Alabama, State, Public Works Department
Atlantic City, Air Control, Department (of)
Austria, Republic (of), Tourism, Department (of)
Buffalo, City, Sanitation, Department (of)
United States Government, Health (and) Human Services, Department (of)

Practice 4: Code the unarranged names below. Then place them in alphabetic order.

Unarranged Names	Alphabetic Order
South Dakota Bureau of Finance and Management	_____
	_____
South Carolina Department of Insurance	_____
	_____
U.S. Department of Agriculture	_____
	_____
Syracuse Street Maintenance Department	_____
	_____
U.S. Department of Commerce	_____
	_____

Code the unarranged names below and then put them in alphabetic order.

Unarranged Names

1. San Diego Dept. of Highways

2. St. Louis Dry Goods Corp.

3. Louis' Bakery Shops, Inc.

4. Selma Diego & Sons, Truckers

5. Kansas City Boutiques, Inc.

6. Republic of Santo Domingo, Ministry of Education

7. Kansas City Dept. of Welfare

8. New York State Bureau of Public Affairs

Alphabetic Order

_____

_____

_____

_____

_____

_____

_____

_____

_____

_____

_____

_____

WHAT HAVE YOU LEARNED IN SECTION 1?

(1) U.S. government names are indexed so that the first three units are <u>United States Government</u>, even if the word <u>Government</u> does not appear in the name.

(2) Any name having to do with a state, county, or city government is indexed with the name of that state, county, or city first. The words <u>State</u>, <u>County</u>, or <u>City</u> are included, even if they are not mentioned in the name, and are indexed separately.

(3) A foreign government name is indexed with the name of the country as the first unit.

(4) Any word that describes a government office, such as <u>Ministry</u>, <u>Department</u>, or <u>Bureau</u>, is a separate indexing unit. The word <u>of</u> is disregarded in indexing but is placed in parentheses.

SECTION 2   GOVERNMENT NAMES WITH MORE THAN ONE SUBDIVISION

You have learned to index government names with one subdivision (department, ministry, or bureau). However, you will usually find that there is more than one subdivision in a government name.

The order of these subdivisions is based on the size of the subdivision. The largest one would usually be a department, and the smallest one would be a board.

DEPARTMENT

BUREAU

DIVISION

COMMISSION

BOARD

Go From the Largest to the Smallest Subdivision

When you index any of these subdivisions, always write the subdivision word (department, bureau, board, etc.) as a separate unit. The word *of* is disregarded but is put in parentheses. Go from the largest to the smallest subdivision in a particular name. Here are some examples:

Unarranged Names

1. Dept. of the Interior, Bureau of Mines
2. Bureau of Labor Statistics, U.S. Department of Labor
3. Customs Bureau, U.S. Treasury Department

Indexing Order

Unit 1	Unit 2	Unit 3	Unit 4	Unit 5	Unit 6	Unit 7	Unit 8
United	States	Government	Interior	Department (of the)	Mines	Bureau (of)	
United	States	Government	Labor	Department (of)	Labor	Statistics	Bureau (of)
United	States	Government	Treasury	Department	Customs	Bureau	

The alphabetic order of such government names would follow in the usual way from unit to unit.

Remember!
For All Federal Government Names:

Now you are ready to index and alphabetize government names with more than one subdivision. The unarranged names below have been indexed. Then they have been placed in alphabetic order.

Unarranged Names

1. Hawaii Dept. of Regulatory Agencies, Insurance Division
2. Dairy and Food Division, Washington Dept. of Agriculture
3. Board of Education, Arkansas Dept. of Education
4. Bureau of Weights, Department of Consumer Affairs, Augusta
5. Akron Public Utilities Commission

Indexing Order

	Unit 1	Unit 2	Unit 3	Unit 4	Unit 5	Unit 6	Unit 7
1.	Hawaii	State	Regulatory	Agencies	Department (of)	Insurance	Division
2.	Washington	State	Agriculture	Department (of)	Dairy (and)	Food	Division
3.	Arkansas	State	Education	Department (of)	Education	Board (of)	
4.	Augusta	City	Consumer	Affairs	Department (of)	Weights	Bureau (of)
5.	Akron	City	Public	Utilities	Commission		

Alphabetic Order

Akron, City, Public Utilities Commission
Arkansas, State, Education, Department (of), Education, Board (of)
Augusta, City, Consumer Affairs, Department (of), Weights, Bureau (of)
Hawaii, State, Regulatory Agencies, Department (of), Insurance Division
Washington, State, Agriculture, Department (of), Dairy (and) Food Division

Practice 1: Index the unarranged names below. Then place them in alphabetic order.

Unarranged Names

1. U.S. Bureau of the Census, Dept. of Commerce
2. Bureau of the Mint, U.S. Dept. of the Treasury
3. New York City Legal Division, Dept. of Corrections
4. City Collections Bureau, Newark Finance Dept.
5. Bureau of Buildings, San Diego Dept. of Housing
6. Republic of Brazil, Dept. of Commerce, Customs Bureau

Indexing Order

	Unit 1	Unit 2	Unit 3	Unit 4	Unit 5	Unit 6	Unit 7
1.	_____	_____	_____	_____	_____	_____	_____
2.	_____	_____	_____	_____	_____	_____	_____
3.	_____	_____	_____	_____	_____	_____	_____
4.	_____	_____	_____	_____	_____	_____	_____
5.	_____	_____	_____	_____	_____	_____	_____
6.	_____	_____	_____	_____	_____	_____	_____

Alphabetic Order

_____

_____

_____

_____

_____

_____

_____

_____

_____

_____

The unarranged names below have been indexed. Then they have been placed in alphabetic order in the list of names below.

Unarranged Names

1. Vocational Division, New Jersey State Education Dept.
2. Alabama State Employment Division, Dept. of Labor

Indexing Order

	Unit 1	Unit 2	Unit 3	Unit 4	Unit 5	Unit 6	Unit 7
1.	New	Jersey	State	Education	Department	Vocational	Division
2.	Alabama	State	Labor	Department (of)	Employment	Division	

Alphabetic Order

Alabama, State, Labor, Department (of), Employment Division

Florida, State, Public Services, Department (of), Fire Control, Bureau (of)

Fulton, City, Public Services, Department (of), Parks, Division (of)

New Jersey, State, Education Department, Vocational Division

New York City, Finance, Department (of), Income Tax, Bureau (of)

Practice 2: Index the unarranged names and then place them in alphabetic order in the list below.

Unarranged Names

1. Troy Bureau of Welfare, Dept. of Public Assistance
2. Michigan Dept. of Transportation, Division of Traffic

Indexing Order

	Unit 1	Unit 2	Unit 3	Unit 4	Unit 5	Unit 6	Unit 7
1.	_____	_____	_____	_____	_____	_____	_____
	_____	_____	_____	_____	_____	_____	_____
2.	_____	_____	_____	_____	_____	_____	_____
	_____	_____	_____	_____	_____	_____	_____

Alphabetic Order

Buffalo, City, Health, Department (of), Hospitals, Bureau (of)

Chicago, City, Commerce, Department (of), Trade, Bureau (of)

Ohio, State, Labor, Department (of), Unemployment, Division (of)

The unarranged names below have been indexed. If the indexing order is *correct*, a check mark has been placed in the *Right* column. If the indexing order is *not* correct, a check mark has been placed in the *Wrong* column.

Unarranged Names

1. Civil Rights Division, U.S. Dept. of Justice
2. U.S. Dept. of Labor, Women's Bureau
3. Idaho State Dept. of Transportation, Bureau of Motor Vehicles

Indexing Order

Unit 1	Unit 2	Unit 3	Unit 4	Unit 5	Unit 6	Unit 7		Right	Wrong
United	States	Justice	Department (of)	Civil	Rights	Division	1.	_____	✓
United	States	Women('s)	Bureau	Labor	Department (of)		2.	_____	✓
Idaho	State	Transportation	Department (of)	Motor	Vehicles	Bureau (of)	3.	✓	_____

Practice 3: The unarranged names below have been indexed. If the indexing order is *correct*, place a check mark in the *Right* column. If the indexing order is *not* correct, place a check mark in the *Wrong* column.

Unarranged Names

1. Baltimore Dept. of Public Welfare, Division of Parks
2. California Dept. of Health, Bureau of Narcotics Control
3. St. Paul Dept. of Traffic, Division of Safety
4. El Paso Dept. of Health, Division of Hospitals
5. Illinois Dept. of Finance, Estate Bureau

Indexing Order

Unit 1	Unit 2	Unit 3	Unit 4	Unit 5	Unit 6	Unit 7
Baltimore	City	Welfare	Public	Department (of)	Parks	Division (of)
California	State	Health	Department (of)	Narcotics	Control	Bureau (of)
St. Paul	Safety	Division (of)	Traffic	Department (of)		
El Paso	Hospitals	Division (of)	Health	Department (of)		
Illinois	State	Finance	Department (of)	Estate	Bureau	

Answers

	Right	Wrong
1.	_____	_____
2.	_____	_____
3.	_____	_____
4.	_____	_____
5.	_____	_____

Integrated Practice O: Code the unarranged names below and then put them in alphabetic order.

Unarranged Names

1. Vermont Dept. of Taxes

2. Iowa Dept. of Public Safety

3. George Davis, Inc.

4. U.S. Dept. of Justice, Tax Division

5. Georgia Fabric Co., Inc.

6. Georgetown Dept. of Public Service, Division of Libraries

7. St. George Shirt Co.

8. U.S. Dept. of Justice, Antitrust Division

Alphabetic Order

_____

_____

_____

_____

_____

_____

_____

_____

_____

_____

_____

_____

_____

_____

_____

_____

WHAT HAVE YOU LEARNED IN SECTION 2?

(1) Government names may be divided into many parts, or subdivisions.
(2) In indexing government names with more than one subdivision, start with the name of the federal, state, or foreign government.
(3) The order of indexing is from the largest subdivision to the smallest in this order: Department, Bureau, Division, Commission, Board.

SECTION 3   NAMES OF BANKS

There are banks in almost every town and city. Many of these banks have branches in the same town or city. When there are several branch banks of the same name in the same town or city, alphabetic order is determined by the branch names. For example:

Westwood Bank and Trust (First Street Branch)
Westwood Bank and Trust (Plaza Mall Branch)

Some banks have branches in different cities and towns in the same state. When bank names are exactly the same, the *city* names determine the alphabetic order. For example:

State Savings and Loan (Newark, New Jersey)
State Savings and Loan (Trenton, New Jersey)

It is also possible for banks in different parts of the country to have the same names even though they have no connection with each other. Here are some examples:

National Bank of Houston (Houston, Texas)
National Bank of Sacramento (Sacramento, California)
National Bank of Seattle (Seattle, Washington)

Names of banks are indexed in the same order as the names are written. The names of the banks above would be indexed as follows:

	Indexing Order			
Unarranged Names	**Unit 1**	**Unit 2**	**Unit 3**	**Unit 4**
National Bank of Houston (Houston, Texas)	National	Bank (of)	Houston	Texas
National Bank of Sacramento (Sacramento, California)	National	Bank (of)	Sacramento	California
National Bank of Seattle (Seattle, Washington)	National	Bank (of)	Seattle	Washington

Sometimes you may find that the name of the bank and the name of the city are the same for two different banks, such as:

Union Bank of Miami, Florida
Union Bank of Miami, Ohio
Royal Savings Bank of Rome, Georgia
Royal Savings Bank of Rome, New York

In these cases the *state* names determine the alphabetic order.

When indexing names of banks, follow these rules:

(1) Index bank names in the same order as they are written.

(2) When bank names are identical, determine alphabetic order first by city, and then by state.

(3) Consider branch bank names only after comparing the bank, city, and state names.

(4) If the name of the bank contains a geographic location, index the location only once. For example, *Los Angeles National Bank* (Los Angeles, California) would be indexed as follows:

Indexing Order

Unit 1	Unit 2	Unit 3	Unit 4
Los Angeles	National	Bank	California

The unarranged names below have been indexed and then placed in alphabetic order.

Indexing Order

Unarranged Names	Unit 1	Unit 2	Unit 3	Unit 4	Unit 5	Unit 6
Union Bank of Miami (Miami, Florida)	Union	Bank (of)	Miami	Florida		
Union Bank of Atlanta (Atlanta, Georgia)	Union	Bank (of)	Atlanta	Georgia		
Federal Savings Bank of Rome, Georgia	Federal	Savings	Bank (of)	Rome	Georgia	
Federal Savings Bank of Rome, New York	Federal	Savings	Bank (of)	Rome	New	York

Alphabetic Order

Federal Savings Bank (of) Rome, Georgia
Federal Savings Bank (of) Rome, New York
Union Bank (of) Atlanta (Atlanta, Georgia)
Union Bank (of) Miami (Miami, Florida)

Practice 1: Index the unarranged names below. Then place them in alphabetic order.

Indexing Order

Unarranged Names	Unit 1	Unit 2	Unit 3	Unit 4	Unit 5	Unit 6
Community Savings Bank of Jackson, Mississippi	_____	_____	_____	_____	_____	_____
First Trust Co. of Albany, New York	_____	_____	_____	_____	_____	_____
Community Savings Bank of Jackson, Kansas	_____	_____	_____	_____	_____	_____
First Trust Co. of Albany, Georgia	_____	_____	_____	_____	_____	_____

Alphabetic Order

_____

_____

_____

_____

Notice that the unarranged names below have been indexed and then placed in alphabetic order in the list of names below.

Unarranged Names

1. City Savings & Loan Association of Chicago, Illinois
2. Chicago Savings & Loan Association (Chicago, Illinois)

Indexing Order

Unit 1	Unit 2	Unit 3	Unit 4	Unit 5	Unit 6
1. City	Savings (&)	Loan	Association (of)	Chicago	Illinois
2. Chicago	Savings (&)	Loan	Association	Illinois	

Alphabetic Order

Chicago Bank (for) Savings (Chicago, Illinois)

Chicago Savings Bank (&) Trust Company (Chicago, Illinois)

Chicago Savings (&) Loan Association (Chicago, Illinois)

Chicago State Loan Bank (Chicago, Illinois)

City Savings (&) Loan Association (of) Chicago, Illinois

Practice 2: Index the unarranged names below. Then place them in alphabetic order in the list of names below.

Unarranged Names

1. County Savings Bank of Detroit, Michigan
2. East Detroit Savings & Loan Association (Detroit, Michigan)

Indexing Order

Unit 1	Unit 2	Unit 3	Unit 4	Unit 5	Unit 6
1. _____	_____	_____	_____	_____	_____
2. _____	_____	_____	_____	_____	_____

Alphabetic Order

Detroit Third National Bank (&) Trust Company (Detroit, Michigan)

Detroit Trust Company (Detroit, Michigan)

East Lansing Public Savings Bank (Lansing, Michigan)

Notice that the unarranged names below have been indexed. If the indexing order is *correct*, a check mark has been placed in the *Right* column. If the indexing order is *not* correct, a check mark has been placed in the *Wrong* column. Then the incorrectly indexed name has been written in correct indexing order below.

Unarranged Names

1. Standard Bank of Cleveland, Ohio
2. United States Trust Co. (Cincinnati, Ohio)
3. United Savings & Loan Co. of Cleveland, Ohio

Indexing Order

	Unit 1	Unit 2	Unit 3	Unit 4	Unit 5	Unit 6	Right	Wrong
1.	Cleveland	Bank (of)	Standard	Ohio				✓
2.	United	States	Trust	Company	Cincinnati	Ohio	✓	
3.	United	Savings (&)	Loan	Company (of)	Cleveland	Ohio	✓	

Corrected Indexing Order

Unit 1	Unit 2	Unit 3	Unit 4	Unit 5	Unit 6
Standard	*Bank (of)*	*Cleveland*	*Ohio*		

Practice 3: The unarranged names below have been indexed. If the indexing order is *correct*, place a check mark in the *Right* column. If the indexing order is *not* correct, place a check mark in the *Wrong* column. Then write the incorrectly indexed name in correct indexing order below.

Unarranged Names

1. Third Federal Trust Co. of Philadelphia (Philadelphia, Pennsylvania)
2. First Federal Bank & Trust Co. of Pittsburgh (Pittsburgh, Pennsylvania)
3. Pittsburg Peoples Bank (Pittsburg, Kansas)
4. Augusta Trust Association (Augusta, Maine)

Indexing Order

	Unit 1	Unit 2	Unit 3	Unit 4	Unit 5	Unit 6	Right	Wrong
1.	Philadelphia	Third	Federal	Trust	Company	Pennsylvania		
2.	First	Federal	Bank (&)	Trust	Company	Pennsylvania		
3.	Pittsburg	Peoples	Bank	Kansas				
4.	Augusta	Trust	Association	Maine				

Corrected Indexing Order

	Unit 1	Unit 2	Unit 3	Unit 4	Unit 5	Unit 6	Unit 7
1.							
2.							
3.							
4.							

The unarranged names below have been coded. Then they have been placed in alphabetic order.

Unarranged Names

    1   2   3   4
Paris South Side Trust Company
(Paris, Georgia)
    1   2   3   4
Paris Federal Trust Company
(Paris, Kentucky)
    1   2   3   4   5
Paris Suburban Federal Trust Company
(Paris, Tennessee)
    1   2   3   4
Portland Bank (&) Trust Company
(Portland, Maine)

Alphabetic Order

Paris Federal Trust Company (Paris, Kentucky)
Paris South Side Trust Company (Paris, Georgia)
Paris Suburban Federal Trust Company (Paris, Tennessee)
Portland Bank (&) Trust Company (Portland, Maine)

Practice 4: Code the unarranged names below. Then place them in alphabetic order.

Unarranged Names	**Alphabetic Order**
Adams Savings Bank (Adams, Massachusetts)	_____
Adams National State Bank (Adams, Massachusetts)	_____
Jackson Dime Savings & Loan Association (Jackson, Mississippi)	_____
Nickel Savings Bank (Jackson, Michigan)	_____

Unarranged Names

1. Security National Bank of Charlotte (Charlotte, North Carolina)

2. Nevada Dept. of Mines, Bureau of Safety

3. North-East Freight Rentals, Inc.

4. R. C. Tyler & Sons, Inc.

5. National Bank of Reno (Reno, Nevada)

6. U.S. Dept. of the Interior, Bureau of Mines

7. Nickel Savings Bank of Norfolk, Nebraska

Alphabetic Order

_____

_____

_____

_____

_____

_____

_____

_____

WHAT HAVE YOU LEARNED IN SECTION 3?

(1) Bank names are indexed and alphabetized in the order in which the names are written.
(2) If the names of banks are the same, the town or city names determine the alphabetic order.
(3) If the bank names and the town or city names are the same, the state names determine the alphabetic order.
(4) Branch bank names are considered only after comparing the bank, city, and state names.
(5) If the name of the bank contains a geographic location, the location is indexed only once.

SECTION 4   NAMES OF CHAIN STORES

You have probably seen stores in different parts of a city that have exactly the same name. That is because they are part of one business firm. Such stores are called branches or *chain stores*.

If many stores in the same state have the same name, the name of the *city* determines the alphabetic order. When stores with the same name are in the same city, the *street address* determines the alphabetic order.

Here are some store names that are alike except for the city:

	Indexing Order	
Unarranged Names	**Unit 1**	**Unit 2**
Reliance Stores (Portland)	Reliance	Stores (Portland)
Reliance Stores (Plainfield)	Reliance	Stores (Plainfield)
Reliance Stores (Perry)	Reliance	Stores (Perry)

As you can see, the name of the store is indexed as Units 1 and 2. The name of the city is put in parentheses and is *not* counted as an indexing unit. Since the names of the stores are the same, however, you would use the name of the city to decide the alphabetic order.

When the store names and the city names are the same, use the *state name* to decide the alphabetic order. Here is an example:

	Indexing Order		
Unarranged Names	**Unit 1**	**Unit 2**	**Unit 3**
Hanover Dress Shops (Albany, Georgia)	Hanover	Dress	Shops (Albany, Georgia)
Hanover Dress Shops (Albany, New York)	Hanover	Dress	Shops (Albany, New York)
Hanover Dress Shops (Albany, Oregon)	Hanover	Dress	Shops (Albany, Oregon)

In this case, the state name decides the alphabetic order.

When stores with the same name are in the same city and the same state, the street name is used to decide the alphabetic order. Here is an example:

Unarranged Names

1. Specialty Stores (182 South Street, Houston, Texas)
2. Specialty Stores (35 Main Street, Houston, Texas)

Indexing Order

Unit 1	Unit 2
1. Specialty	Stores (Houston, Texas, South Street, 182)
2. Specialty	Stores (Houston, Texas, Main Street, 35)

In the names above, the store names, city names, and state names are the same. Therefore, you would use the name of the street to decide the alphabetic order, with *Main* coming before *South*.

Look carefully at how the *address* was written:

Unarranged Addresses	Order of Consideration
182 South Street, Houston, Texas	(Houston, Texas, South Street, 182)
35 Main Street, Houston, Texas	(Houston, Texas, Main Street, 35)

The city is always the first part of the address to be considered when the store names are the same. The state name is considered next, then the street name, and finally the street number.

When there are stores with the same name in the same city and on the same street, use the number part of the address to decide alphabetic order. Here is an example:

Unarranged Names

1. Union Pet Stores (315 Broadway, New York, New York)
2. Union Pet Stores (1482 Broadway, New York, New York)

Indexing Order

Unit 1	Unit 2	Unit 3
1. Union	Pet	Stores (New York, New York, Broadway, 315)
2. Union	Pet	Stores (New York, New York, Broadway, 1482)

Since the street names are the same, consider the number part of the address and decide alphabetic order numerically. By putting the smaller number first, *315* Broadway comes before *1482* Broadway. Notice that in this case alphabetic order is *not* decided by spelling out the number.

Now you are ready to index and alphabetize the names of chain stores. The unarranged names below have been indexed. Then they have been placed in alphabetic order.

Unarranged Names

1. Fashion Boutique Stores (115 Main Street, Hartford, Connecticut)
2. Fashion Boutique Stores (Salem, Illinois)
3. Fashion Boutique Stores (Salem, Massachusetts)
4. Fashion Boutique Stores (27 Main Street, Hartford, Connecticut)

Indexing Order

Unit 1	Unit 2	Unit 3
1. Fashion	Boutique	Stores (Hartford, Connecticut, Main Street, 115)
2. Fashion	Boutique	Stores (Salem, Illinois)
3. Fashion	Boutique	Stores (Salem, Massachusetts)
4. Fashion	Boutique	Stores (Hartford, Connecticut, Main Street, 27)

Alphabetic Order

Fashion Boutique Stores (27 Main Street, Hartford, Connecticut)
Fashion Boutique Stores (115 Main Street, Hartford, Connecticut)
Fashion Boutique Stores (Salem, Illinois)
Fashion Boutique Stores (Salem, Massachusetts)

Practice 1: Index the unarranged names below. Then place them in alphabetic order.

Unarranged Names

1. Wellman Stores (Augusta, Maine)
2. Wellman Stores (Augusta, Georgia)
3. Wellman Stores (401 Davis Street, Richmond, Virginia)
4. Wellman Stores (177 Davis Street, Richmond, Virginia)
5. Wellman Stores (27 Oak Avenue, Richmond, Virginia)

Indexing Order

Unit 1	Unit 2
1. _____	_____
2. _____	_____
3. _____	_____
4. _____	_____
5. _____	_____

Alphabetic Order

_____
_____
_____
_____
_____

In the example below the unarranged names have been indexed. Then they have been placed in alphabetic order in the list of names.

Unarranged Names

1. Boswell Stores (226 State Street, Auburn, Alabama)
2. Boswell Stores (Auburn, Texas)

Indexing Order

Unit 1	Unit 2
1. Boswell	Stores (Auburn, Alabama, State Street, 226)
2. Boswell	Stores (Auburn, Texas)

Alphabetic Order

Boswell Stores (82 Adams Street, Auburn, Alabama)

Boswell Stores (226 State Street, Auburn, Alabama)

Boswell Stores (836 State Street, Auburn, Alabama)

Boswell Stores (Auburn, Texas)

Boswell Stores (Birmingham, Alabama)

Practice 2: Index the unarranged names below. Then place them in alphabetic order in the list below.

Unarranged Names

1. Clinton Shops (12 Elm Street, Gary, Indiana)
2. Clinton Shops (Ames, Iowa)

Indexing Order

Unit 1	Unit 2
1. _____	_____
2. _____	_____

Alphabetic Order

Clinton Shops (Albany, Georgia)

Clinton Shops (406 Broad Street, Gary, Indiana)

Clinton Shops (362 Elm Street, Gary, Indiana)

The unarranged names below have been placed in indexing order. If the indexing order is *correct*, a check mark has been placed in the *Right* column. If the indexing order is *not* correct, a check mark has been placed in the *Wrong* column. Then the incorrectly indexed name has been written in correct indexing order below.

Unarranged Names

1. Leslie Luggage Shops (23 Cambridge Street, Baltimore, Maryland)
2. Leslie Luggage Shops (Kansas City, Missouri)
3. Leslie Luggage Shops (44 Tyler Road, Baltimore, Maryland)

		Indexing Order	Answers	
Unit 1	**Unit 2**	**Unit 3**	**Right**	**Wrong**
1. Leslie	Luggage	Shops (Cambridge, 23 Street, Baltimore, Maryland)	_____	✓
2. Leslie	Luggage	Shops (Kansas City, Missouri)	✓	_____
3. Leslie	Luggage	Shops (Baltimore, Maryland, Tyler Road, 44)	✓	_____

Corrected Indexing Order

Unit 1	**Unit 2**	**Unit 3**
Leslie	Luggage	Shops (Baltimore, Maryland, Cambridge Street, 23)

Practice 3: The unarranged names below have been indexed. If the indexing order is *correct*, place a check mark in the *Right* column. If the indexing order is *not* correct, place a check mark in the *Wrong* column. Then write the incorrectly indexed names in correct indexing order below.

Unarranged Names

1. Mohawk Tire Co. (24 Foster Road, Dayton, Ohio)
2. Mohawk Tire Co. (29 Drew Avenue, Hollywood, Florida)
3. Mohawk Tire Co. (Hollywood, California)
4. Mohawk Tire Co. (88 Grand Road, Dayton, Ohio)

		Indexing Order	Answers	
Unit 1	**Unit 2**	**Unit 3**	**Right**	**Wrong**
1. Mohawk	Tire	Company (Dayton, Ohio, Foster Road, 24)	_____	_____
2. Hollywood	Florida	(Mohawk Tire Company, 29 Drew Avenue)	_____	_____
3. Mohawk	Tire	Company (Hollywood, California)	_____	_____
4. Mohawk	Tire	Company (Dayton, Ohio, Grand Road, 88)	_____	_____

Corrected Indexing Order

Unit 1	**Unit 2**	**Unit 3**
_____	_____	_____
_____	_____	_____
_____	_____	_____
_____	_____	_____

The unarranged names below have been coded. Then they have been placed in alphabetic order.

Unarranged Names

1   2   3
Freehold Cleaners, Inc. (66 Evans Road, Norfolk, Virginia)

1   2   3
Freehold Cleaners, Inc. (41 Main Street, Norfolk, Virginia)

1   2   3
Freehold Cleaners, Inc. (168 Archer Street, Norfolk, Virginia)

1   2   3
Freehold Cleaners, Inc. (1711 Fenway Street, Norfolk, Virginia)

1   2   3
Freehold Cleaners, Inc. (85 Drake Avenue, Shreveport, Louisiana)

1   2   3
Freehold Cleaners, Inc. (372 Drake Avenue, Shreveport, Louisiana)

Alphabetic Order

Freehold Cleaners, Inc. (168 Archer Street, Norfolk, Virginia)
Freehold Cleaners, Inc. (66 Evans Road, Norfolk, Virginia)
Freehold Cleaners, Inc. (1711 Fenway Street, Norfolk, Virginia)
Freehold Cleaners, Inc. (41 Main Street, Norfolk, Virginia)
Freehold Cleaners, Inc. (85 Drake Avenue, Shreveport, Louisiana)
Freehold Cleaners, Inc. (372 Drake Avenue, Shreveport, Louisiana)

When two business names are the same, use their geographic locations to decide alphabetic order.

Practice 4: Code the unarranged names below. Then place them in alphabetic order.

Unarranged Names

Pembrook Shirt Co. (52 Fulton Street, Frankfort, Kentucky)

Pembrook Shirt Co. (575 Center Street, Frankfort, Kentucky)

Pembrook Shirt Co. (101 Gary Street, Frankfort, Kentucky)

Pembrook Shirt Co. (49 Greene Street, Lafayette, Louisiana)

Pembrook Shirt Co. (268 Greene Street, Lafayette, Indiana)

Alphabetic Order

_____

_____

_____

_____

_____

When business names and city and state names are the same, use the street name to decide alphabetic order.

Integrated Practice Q: Code the unarranged names below and then put them in alphabetic order.

Unarranged Names

1. Dollar National Bank of Dover, Delaware
2. Dollar Discount Stores (Dover, New Jersey)
3. Dollar Discount Stores (Dover, Delaware)
4. C. G. Dollar & Sons, Inc.

5. C D Stores, Inc.
6. U.S. Dept. of Defense, Navy Dept.
7. North West Book Co.
8. Northern Railways, Inc.

Alphabetic Order

_____
_____
_____
_____
_____
_____
_____
_____
_____

WHAT HAVE YOU LEARNED IN SECTION 4?

(1) When a firm has many stores with the same name, use the location of the store to decide the alphabetic order.

(2) Index chain store names by the name of the firm. The location of the store is put in parentheses after the last unit.

(3) If store names are the same, use the city name to decide alphabetic order.

(4) If store names and city names are the same, use the name of the state to decide alphabetic order.

(5) If store names, city names, and state names are the same, use the name of the street to decide alphabetic order.

(6) If store names, city names, state names, and street names are the same, use the street number to decide alphabetic order, putting the smallest number first.

SECTION 5 SIMULATED OFFICE PROBLEMS

You have learned how to file folders in the type of cabinet shown on the left below. This type of cabinet is called a *vertical filing cabinet*. Many firms use the type of filing cabinet like the one shown on the right below. This type of cabinet is called a *lateral filing cabinet*.

**Five-Drawer Vertical
Filing Cabinet**

The Shaw-Walker Co.

**Five-Drawer Lateral
Filing Cabinet**

Esselte Pendaflex Corp.

Many lateral file drawers use *hanging* or *suspension* file folders like the one below on the left. When you use hanging folders, the folders hang on a rack that is set inside the drawer. Hanging files keep file folders from sagging or falling down in the drawer. Some people file regular folders inside the hanging folders so that the hanging folders do not have to be removed from the drawer.

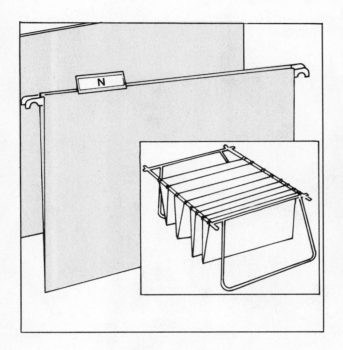

**Hanging Folder
with Rack**

**Lateral File Drawer with
Hanging Folders**

Hanging folders usually have clear plastic tabs which fit over the back edge of the folder. The office worker types the name to be filed on a paper caption, folds the paper, and then slips it into the plastic tab.

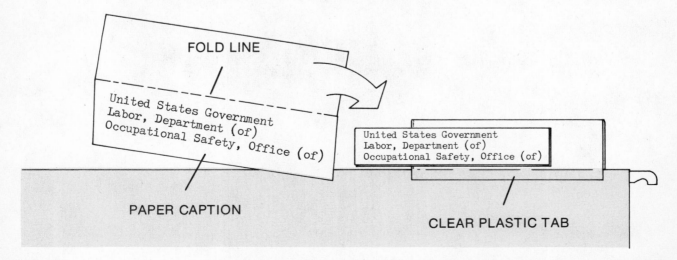

FOLD LINE

United States Government
Labor, Department (of)
Occupational Safety, Office (of)

PAPER CAPTION

United States Government
Labor, Department (of)
Occupational Safety, Office (of)

CLEAR PLASTIC TAB

Notice that the unarranged government names below have been printed in correct indexing order on the folded paper captions at the right.

Folded Paper Captions

Unarranged Names

United States Department of Labor, Office of Occupational Safety

United States Department of Education, Bureau of Adult and Vocational Education

United States Department of the Treasury, Internal Revenue Service, Office of Regional Inspector

United States Department of Agriculture, Office of Audit

United States Government, Labor, Department (of), Occupational Safety, Office (of)

United States Government, Education, Department (of), Adult (and) Vocational Education, Bureau (of)

United States Government, Treasury, Department (of the) Internal Revenue Service, Regional Inspector, Office (of)

United States Government, Agriculture, Department (of), Audit, Office (of)

Practice 1: Print the unarranged names below in correct indexing order on the folded paper captions at the right.

Folded Paper Captions

Unarranged Names

United States Department of Agriculture, Office of Automated Data

United States Department of Labor, Office of Employee Benefits

United States Department of Labor, Office of Veterans' Rights

United States Department of Agriculture, Bureau of Extension Services

United States Department of the Interior, Division of Law Enforcement

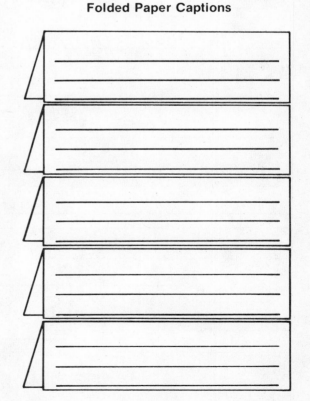

Notice that each unarranged name below was written in indexing order on the lines below the names. Then the indexed names were printed on the correct hanging folder captions in the lateral file drawer.

Unarranged Names

1. Texas Department of Education
   Division of Vocational Education

Texas, State, Education, Department (of), Vocational Education, Division (of)

2. Texas Department of Conservation
   Bureau of Parks

Texas, State, Conservation, Department (of), Parks, Bureau (of)

Texas, State, Vocational
Rehabilitation, Department (of),
Veterans Training, Bureau (of)

Texas, State, Vocational
Rehabilitation, Department (of),
Blind, Bureau (for the)

Texas, State, Labor,
Department (of),
Employment Security, Bureau (of)

Texas, State, Highways,
Department (of),
Highway Inspection, Bureau (of)

Texas, State, Education, Department (of), Vocational Education, Division (of)

Texas, State,
Corrections, Department (of),
Prisons, Bureau (of)

Texas, State, Conservation, Department (of), Parks, Bureau (of)

TEXAS

TEXAS

Practice 2: Write each unarranged name below in indexing order on the lines below the names. Then print the indexed names on the correct hanging folder captions in the lateral file drawer.

Unarranged Names

1. Ohio Department of Education
   Division of Vocational Education

2. Ohio Department of Corrections
   Bureau of Prison Inspection

_____   _____

_____   _____

_____   _____

Ohio, State, Probation and Parole,
Department (of), Field Services,
Bureau (of)

Ohio, State, Hospitals,
Department (of),
Hospitals Inspections, Bureau (of)

Ohio, State, Education,
Department (of),
Teaching Certification, Bureau (of)

Ohio, State, Education,
Department (of),
Adult Education, Bureau (of)

Ohio, State, Child Welfare,
Department (of),
Family Services, Bureau (of)

OHIO

OHIO

Another type of file used in business is called the *shelf file*. In shelf files, file folders are placed on shelves and held up by thin metal dividers which slide into slots on the shelf bottom and back. Some shelf files use small metal bins to hold the folders.

Shelf File

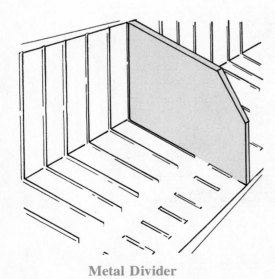

Metal Divider

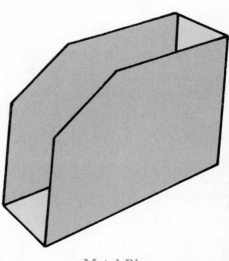

Metal Bin

Guides and folder tabs are often placed on the side so that they are more easily seen in a shelf file. See page 160.

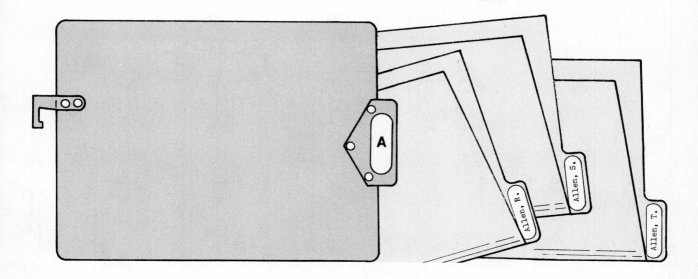

Notice also that the caption is written sideways on the folder tab so that it can be read easily while it is on the shelf.

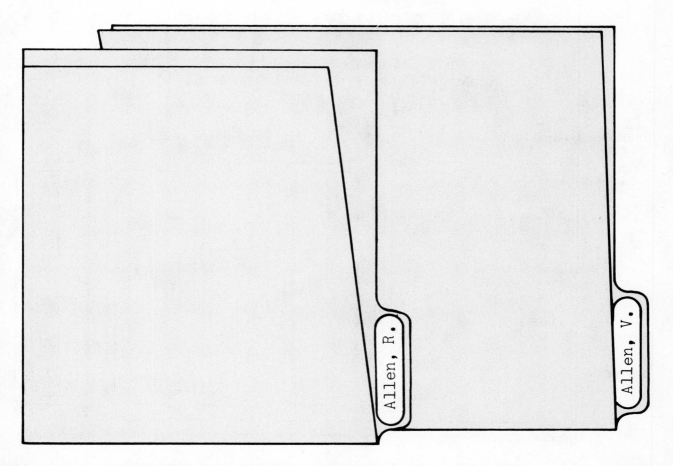

Notice that the unarranged names below were coded. Then they were printed in alphabetic order on the side tab folders for a shelf file.

Unarranged Names

Side Tab Folders

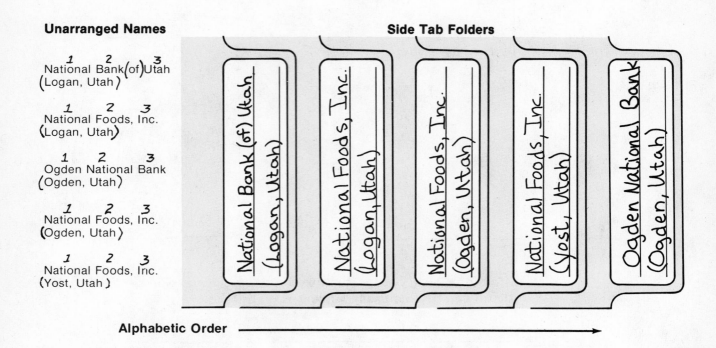

$\overset{1}{\text{National}}$ $\overset{2}{\text{Bank}}$(of)$\overset{3}{\text{Utah}}$
(Logan, Utah)

$\overset{1}{\text{National}}$ $\overset{2}{\text{Foods}}$, $\overset{3}{\text{Inc.}}$
(Logan, Utah)

$\overset{1}{\text{Ogden}}$ $\overset{2}{\text{National}}$ $\overset{3}{\text{Bank}}$
(Ogden, Utah)

$\overset{1}{\text{National}}$ $\overset{2}{\text{Foods}}$, $\overset{3}{\text{Inc.}}$
(Ogden, Utah)

$\overset{1}{\text{National}}$ $\overset{2}{\text{Foods}}$, $\overset{3}{\text{Inc.}}$
(Yost, Utah)

National Bank (of) Utah (Logan, Utah)   National Foods, Inc. (Logan, Utah)   National Foods, Inc. (Ogden, Utah)   National Foods, Inc. (Yost, Utah)   Ogden National Bank (Ogden, Utah)

Alphabetic Order ⟶

Practice 3: Code the unarranged names below. Then print the names in alphabetic order on the side tab folders.

Unarranged Names

Side Tab Folders

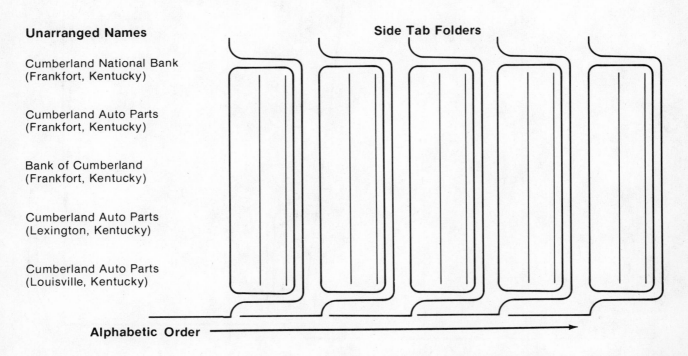

Cumberland National Bank
(Frankfort, Kentucky)

Cumberland Auto Parts
(Frankfort, Kentucky)

Bank of Cumberland
(Frankfort, Kentucky)

Cumberland Auto Parts
(Lexington, Kentucky)

Cumberland Auto Parts
(Louisville, Kentucky)

Alphabetic Order ⟶

Notice that two of the unarranged names below were printed in incorrect indexing order on the tabs of the shelf file folders. The incorrectly indexed names were crossed out and then printed in correct indexing order in the spaces below.

Unarranged Names

Orange National Bank
(Orlando, Florida)

Orlando Fruit Company
(Orlando, Florida)

Orlando Department of Parks
(Orlando, Florida)

Orlando Fruit Company
(Miami, Florida)

National Bank of Orlando
(Orlando, Florida)

Orlando Streets Department
(Orlando, Florida)

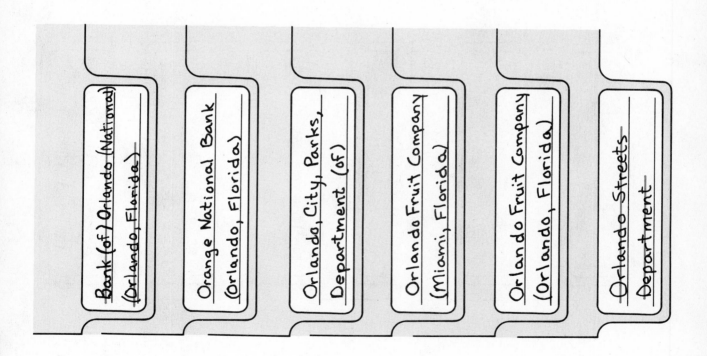

Corrected Indexing Order

1. National Bank (of) Orlando
   (Orlando, Florida)
2. Orlando, City, Streets Department

_____

Practice 4: Two of the unarranged names below were printed in incorrect indexing order on the tabs of the shelf file folders. Find the incorrectly indexed names and cross them out. Then print the names in correct indexing order in the spaces below.

Unarranged Names

First National Bank of Maine
(Portland, Maine)

First National Bank of Portland
(Portland, Maine)

Portland Department of Public Works
(Portland, Maine)

Portland Trading Company
(Portland, Maine)

Portland Fire Department
(Portland, Maine)

Portland Trading Company
(Augusta, Maine)

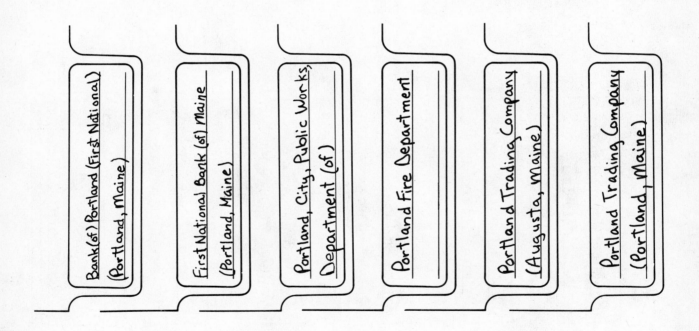

Corrected Indexing Order

1. _____

_____

2. _____

_____